JOURNEY TO TOPAZ

RELATED HEYDAY TITLES:

Samurai of Gold Hill
by Yoshiko Uchida; illustrated by Ati Forberg

Only What We Could Carry:
The Japanese-American Internment Experience
edited by Lawson Fusao Inada

Topaz Moon: Chiura Obata's Art of the Internment
edited by Kimi Kodani Hill

Making Home from War:
Stories of Japanese American Exile and Resettlement
edited by Brian Komei Dempster

Children of Manzanar
edited by Heather C. Lindquist

JOURNEY to TOPAZ

A STORY OF THE JAPANESE-AMERICAN EVACUATION

YOSHIKO UCHIDA

ILLUSTRATED BY DONALD CARRICK

HEYDAY, BERKELEY, CALIFORNIA

In memory of my mother and father
and for my Issei friends

Heyday is thankful for our community of friends and supporters who made this
project possible. For a full list of donors, please visit www.heydaybooks.com.

Library of Congress Cataloging-in-Publication Data
Uchida, Yoshiko.
  Journey to Topaz : a story of the Japanese-American evacuation / by Yoshiko
Uchida ; illustrated by Donald Carrick.
      p. cm.
  Summary: After the Pearl Harbor attack an eleven-year-old Japanese-American
girl and her family are forced to go to an aliens camp in Utah.
  ISBN 978-1-890771-91-1 (pbk. : alk. paper)
  ISBN 1-890771-91-0 (pbk. : alk. paper)
  1. Japanese Americans—Evacuation and relocation, 1942-1945—Juvenile fic-
tion. [1. Japanese Americans—Evacuation and relocation, 1942-1945—Fiction.
2. World War, 1939-1945—United States--Fiction.] I. Carrick, Donald, ill. II.
Title.
  PZ7.U25Jo 2005
  [Fic]—dc22

                                            2004016537

Printed in Saline, MI, by McNaughton and Gunn
Orders, inquiries, and correspondence should be addressed to:
        Heyday
        P. O. Box 9145, Berkeley, CA 94709
        (510) 549-3564, Fax (510) 549-1889
        www.heydaybooks.com

20 19 18 17 16 15

FSC
www.fsc.org
MIX
Paper from
responsible sources
FSC® C011935

Prologue

It has been many years since I first wrote *Journey to Topaz* and more than forty years since the United States government uprooted 120,000 West Coast Japanese Americans, without trial or hearing, and imprisoned them behind barbed wire. Two-thirds of those Japanese Americans were American citizens, and I was one of them. We were imprisoned by our own country during World War II, not because of anything we had done, but simply because we looked like the enemy.

Today we know, in spite of the government claim at the time, that there was no military necessity for this action. Today we know this gross violation of our Constitution caused one of the most shameful episodes in our country's history. Our leaders betrayed not only the Japanese Americans, but *all* Americans, for by denying the Constitution, they damaged the very essence of our democratic beliefs.

In 1976 President Gerald R. Ford stated, "Not only was that evacuation wrong, but Japanese Americans were and are loyal Americans . . . we have learned from the tragedy of that long-ago experience forever to treasure liberty and justice for each individual American." In 1983 a Commission of Wartime Relocation and Internment of Civilians established by the United States Congress concluded that a grave injustice was done to

Japanese Americans and that the causes of the uprooting were race prejudice, war hysteria and a failure of leadership.

Journey to Topaz is the story of what happened to one Japanese American family during this wartime tragedy, then called "the evacuation." Although the characters are fictional, the events are based on actual fact, and most of what happened to the Sakane family also happened to my own.

I would ask readers to remember that my characters portray the Japanese Americans of 1942 and to recall that the world then was totally different from the one we know today. In 1942 the voice of Martin Luther King had not yet been heard and ethnic pride was yet unborn. There was no awareness in the land of civil rights, and there had yet been no freedom marches or demonstrations of protest. Most Americans, supporting their country in a war they considered just, did nothing to protest our forced removal, and might well have considered it treasonous had we tried to resist or protest.

Told to demonstrate our loyalty by doing as our country asked, we had no choice but to trust our government leaders. We did not know then, as we do now, that they had acceded to political and economic pressure groups and imprisoned us with full knowledge that their action was not only unconstitutional, but totally unnecessary.

I hope by reading this book young people everywhere will realize what once took place in this country and will determine never to permit such a travesty of justice to occur again.

Yoshiko Uchida
Berkeley, California
January 1984

Contents

1

Strangers at the Door

$\mathcal{I}$T was only the first week in December, but already Yuki could feel the tingling excitement of Christmas in the air. There was, of course, no sign of snow, for it never snowed in Berkeley except for the winter when she was six and a thin flurry of flakes had surprised them all. Yuki remembered how she had run outside, stretched her arms wide and opened her mouth, thrusting out her tongue so she could feel the snow and taste it and gather it to her in any way she could before the flakes reached the ground and disappeared. Today looked like snow weather for the sky was gray and murky, but only with fog that blew in cold and damp from San Francisco Bay.

Yuki stood close to the fireplace with its burning oak logs and lifted her skirt to feel the warmth as she waited for Mother to fix lunch. On such a cold gloomy Sunday, it felt especially good to be close to a fire and think glowing thoughts about Christmas. It

1

wouldn't be long before a tall fir tree with its fresh green forest smell would be standing in the corner of the living room and the kitchen would be filled with the wonderful scent of Mother's butter cookies.

Yuki thought happily of the presents that would soon gather under the tree. She had already decided to get Mother a soft blue chiffon scarf to go with her Sunday church coat, some wool socks for Father and maybe a tie or a record for her older brother, Ken. It was hardest to find something good for Ken. Now that he was going to the university, he seemed to live in a changed world and to be almost a different person. He was eighteen and suddenly it was no longer football and baseball and basketball alone that fascinated him. He liked girls.

"I'm a girl," Yuki reminded him periodically. "Why don't you take me to the movies?"

But Ken only laughed. "I like girls over sixteen," he explained. "You've still got five years to go, and besides that, you're my sister. That makes you an entirely different specimen altogether!"

Yuki sometimes looked at herself in the mirror, wrinkling her nose at the round full face and the straight black hair that fell to her shoulders. She would push aside her bangs and contemplate the possibilities. How would she look when she was sixteen anyway? Not very good, she decided, but she wasn't going to let that bother her, at least for now.

"Yuki Chan!" Mother roused Yuki from her reveries about Christmas and her older brother. "Lunch is ready. Will you go outside and call your father?"

Yuki hurried toward the back door, stopping on the way to

2

get some dog biscuits for Pepper. Father was out in the yard tying up the last of the white chrysanthemums and burning old leaves. He hadn't been home from church an hour and already he was hard at work outdoors where he loved to be.

Father went to church each Sunday because he believed it was the proper thing to do. He didn't read the Bible each day as Mother did, and Yuki wasn't even sure he said his prayers every night before going to sleep. In fact, she suspected that if he had his way, he would have preferred working in his garden on Sundays to sitting in the small dark Japanese church in Oakland listening to Reverend Wada, their minister from Japan, and hearing the drone of the reed organ wheezing out the seemingly endless hymns. "You know," he had once said to Mother, "sometimes God seems closer out there in the fresh air with the flowers and trees than in that sanctuary." But when he talked like that, Mother wouldn't even dignify his comment with an answer.

As Yuki went out the back door, Pepper came bounding up the steps to meet her, barking and wagging his tail and running in circles around her. He knew Yuki had some biscuits for him, just as he knew that Mother or Father or Ken would. They all spoiled Pepper terribly, but in return, Pepper gave them every ounce of love that he had stored in his lively black body.

"Down Pepper!" Yuki commanded, and then, still playing with Pepper, she shouted to her father. "Come on in, Papa. Lunch is ready."

Father raised his shears to show that he had heard, but he quickly disappeared again behind the chrysanthemums. Yuki knew she'd have to call him at least two more times before he'd

3

even begin to think about coming inside. She took her time, stopping to peer into the fishpond, stirring the water to see if the big gray carp would rise to the surface, his mouth open wide expecting some food. It was a shabby trick, but one that Yuki couldn't resist occasionally just to see if the old carp was alive and alert.

As Yuki studied the murky depths of the fishpond, she heard Mother ringing her small black bell. Mother didn't like shouting to people, so instead she rang her bell and when she did, it meant that everyone should hurry.

Yuki called once more to Father and then ran inside to wash up and set the table with chopsticks, rice bowls, and tea cups. Sunday dinners were usually Japanese meals and Mother would cook a pot of rice in the morning before church and leave it bundled in a quilt on her bed to keep warm. If guests were coming, she would prepare the night before some chicken *teriyaki* and vegetables cooked Japanese style with soy sauce and sugar and ginger. Today, however, there were no guests and Yuki was glad. She wasn't terribly fond of the Japanese students from the seminary who seemed to cluster under Mother's protective wing.

"They're lonely and miss their families in Japan," Mother would explain. But Yuki didn't like the smell of camellia oil that lingered on their thick glossy hair, and she didn't much care for their conversations about the Old Testament or the Sunday sermon. Today, they all had other places to go for Sunday dinner and Ken had gone off to study at the library, so there were only the three of them for dinner.

"Good, no company today," Yuki said cheerfully to her canary, Old Salt. Yuki knew that was not the most appropriate

4

name for a canary, but she had given him that name for Mrs. Jamieson's sake.

Mrs. Jamieson was the widow who lived across the street. When her parrot, Old Salt, had died, she had been so disconsolate that Yuki had been moved to name her own new canary after the parrot.

"Why that's a lovely idea, Yuki dear," Mrs. Jamieson had said brightly, and then quickly added, "Now you'll have a Salt and a Pepper," and she laughed so at her own small joke that she got a stitch in her side and had to sit down.

When Father came in from the garden he turned on the radio before sitting down at the table. Then he gave a short quick grace that fit in nicely just before the voice from the radio filled the room.

"This is a repeat of the news bulletin," a newscaster said harshly, his voice trembling with urgency. "Japanese planes have attacked Pearl Harbor . . . The United States Fleet has been heavily damaged . . . Fires are raging over the waterfront . . ."

Father put down his chopsticks and listened intently. Mother brushed away a piece of hair that had strayed from her bun and pinned it back into place. A frown swept across her pleasant face and she didn't even attempt to eat her lunch. Only Yuki had a mouthful of chicken and sat chewing silently, looking first at Father and then at Mother, trying to understand what had happened.

"It's a terrible mistake, of course," Father said at last. "It must be the work of a fanatic. That is, if it really happened."

Mother agreed. "Of course," she said. "It must be a mistake. Why would Japan ever do such a foolish thing?"

5

They sat in silence, listening in disbelief as the newscaster continued to tell of the attack. Yuki shuddered. The news was like a burden of darkness suddenly blotting out the light of day.

Father turned from the radio and saw the frightened look on Yuki's face. He saw Mother's hands tremble as she picked up her cup of tea, and rising abruptly, he switched off the radio.

"Maybe it is only a drama," he suggested. "Maybe it is not really news at all. In any case, let's not let it spoil our dinner," he said, trying to smile. And pushing his glasses up on his nose, he turned his attention to the food on the table.

Yuki knew, however, that Father was more than a little upset. He always pushed up his glasses when he was disturbed about something, and she knew by his silence that the program had already spoiled his dinner.

It wasn't long before the telephone rang and Father got up to answer it. It was Mr. Toda, one of the men who lived upstairs in the building behind their Japanese church which served as a bachelors' dormitory. Mr. Toda was a frequent Sunday dinner guest too because Mother said he was old and lonely and needed their friendship. He hadn't come today because he thought he was catching a cold.

Yuki liked Mr. Toda better than the seminary students because he was more open about his feelings. If he liked you, he let you know, and if he didn't, he was equally frank. Yuki liked people like that. She knew that the old man liked her too. They were both fond of dogs and birds and fish, and he always had especially pleasant ways of showing his friendship. Whenever he came, he usually brought her small bags of pastel-colored candy that oozed sweet mouthfuls of fruit-flavored juices. Yuki loved the purple grape flavor best and saved those for the last.

Father told Mr. Toda the same thing he'd told Yuki and Mother. It had to be a mistake, he said over and over. And yes, he would surely keep him informed if he heard anything further.

As soon as dinner was over, Father went back to his garden and Mother went to the kitchen to bake a cake. Mother usually baked when she was going to have company or when she was too nervous to settle down to do anything else. Yuki didn't care what prompted her to bake as long as she did it. She made the best cream puffs and chocolate cakes of anyone she knew, Mrs. Jamieson included.

When the doorbell rang, Yuki was sure it must be Michelle Nelson who lived next door. Mimi usually came over on Sunday afternoons to see if she and Yuki could find something interesting to do together.

Yuki ran to the door and flung it open only to find three strange men standing on the porch. They were not Japanese and looked as though they might be business associates of Father's from San Francisco. "Is your father home?" one of them asked. He was not unfriendly, but he did not smile.

Yuki nodded. Then she saw two uniformed policemen come up the stairs behind them.

"Just a minute," she said unsteadily, and leaving the screen door latched, she ran to tell Mother and then rushed outside to call her father.

Father hurried inside and let the men in. He spoke quietly to them and then told Yuki to call Mother.

"These gentlemen are from the FBI," he explained calmly. "It seems the news on the radio was true after all. Japan has attacked Pearl Harbor. They would like me to go with them to answer a few questions. They would also like to search . . . to look

7

around the house," Father said. His voice was strained and the color had drained from his face.

"But why?" Mother asked nervously. "You have done nothing."

"We have orders to apprehend certain men who work for Japanese firms in this area," one of the men answered briefly. "Your husband, Mr. Sakane, is employed by one of Japan's largest business firms."

"I see," Mother said. She was pale and tense.

Yuki could hear the men opening bureau drawers and closet doors. What in the world were they looking for? What did they think Father had hidden?

Soon the men led Father toward the front door. "I am in my gardening clothes," Father explained. "Permit me to change to my business suit."

The men shook their heads. "There isn't time, Mr. Sakane," they said, and they just gave him time to put on a jacket. Father looked small and frail beside the two large FBI men and one took a firm grip on his arm as they went down the steps.

"I'll be back soon," Father said, trying to sound casual. "Don't worry." And then he was gone.

Two of the FBI men went with Father and the third stayed behind, sitting down beside the telephone. The two policemen stayed too. One stood at the front door and the other at the back door.

"We won't try to leave," Mother assured them.

But the policemen told Mother they weren't worried about that. "We have orders not to let anyone in," he explained.

Although the FBI man and the policemen tried to make polite

conversation with her, Yuki didn't feel the least bit friendly. When they asked her name and how old she was, she replied tersely, "Yuki" and "eleven." They had taken Father off like a common criminal and Yuki didn't like it at all.

"Can I go see Mimi?" Yuki asked, looking at Mother but knowing it was the FBI man who would decide.

"Sorry," he said gently, "but you'll have to stay home awhile."

As things turned out, they not only had to stay home, no one could come in or even talk to them by phone. Yuki looked out the window and saw Mimi standing in front of their house, trying to see inside and waving frantically when she caught a glimpse of Yuki's face. She also saw Mrs. Jamieson standing on her front porch peering anxiously in their direction. The telephone rang several times, but to each caller the FBI men simply answered that the Sakanes were indisposed and could not come to the phone.

It was a strange feeling to be a prisoner in one's own home. Still, Yuki felt no fear, for at the time she had no way of knowing that this was only the beginning of a terrible war and that her small comfortable world would soon be turned upside down.

2
The
Long
Wait

THE clock on the mantel ticked noisily in the silence of the living room. The fire had died down leaving only the charred remains of an oak log, but Yuki didn't feel like blowing it back to life. She couldn't settle down to read a book or go to her room to listen to the radio. The house simply didn't feel right with three strange men standing guard over them and sending away friends who came to call.

Yuki wished Ken would come home. Was he still studying at the library not even aware of what had happened?

Yuki wandered listlessly into the kitchen where Mother was now frosting her chocolate cake. She had put a kettle of water on to boil and set out her tea tray on the breakfast room table.

"Who's the tea for?" Yuki asked curiously. "Who's coming?"

Mother always prepared tea when she was expecting visitors. In fact, even if the callers were unexpected she served a pot of fragrant green tea and whatever sweets she had in the lacquer bowl in the cupboard. Anyone who came to their house and stayed for more than ten minutes was always served tea, even the Realsilk Hosiery woman with her bulging bagful of silk underwear and stocking samples.

"No one is coming, Yuki Chan," Mother answered quietly.

"Then who's the tea for?"

"For the policemen and the gentleman from the FBI."

"You're going to give *them* tea and cake?" Yuki asked, dumbfounded. "They're not even friends," she objected. "They took Papa away. Why should you give them any tea?"

Mother quickly brushed aside Yuki's objections. "If we're going to spend the rest of the afternoon with them," she said firmly, "we might just as well be pleasant. After all, they're only doing their duty. We needn't be rude."

Yuki could see that Mother had already made up her mind and there was no use arguing with her. She could be very determined when she wanted to. That was probably why she'd had the courage to come all alone from Japan twenty years ago to marry Father whom she had known only for a short time. "My professors at college knew us both and recommended your father most highly," she had explained once when Yuki asked if she hadn't been worried. That was all she needed. She had come with faith and trust in her heart and she had never been sorry.

Yuki sighed and picked up the tea tray, carrying it into the living room as she usually did when they had guests. Mother would bring the teapot and the cake and do the serving.

The policemen came from their posts and sat down awkwardly on the couch as Mother invited them to have some tea.

Yuki knew they were embarrassed, but they also seemed a little pleased. They relaxed and smiled, and as Yuki sat eating sweet mouthfuls of chocolate cake she could no longer scowl at them. Mother knew it was difficult to have tea and cake with someone and still be unfriendly. Her gentle manner and warm smile, in fact, quickly defrosted anyone who came to their home, even the most haughty or arrogant. Yuki was sure Mother didn't have a single enemy in the whole world, although the rest of them, even Father, had at least one or two.

Each time a car went by, Yuki hurried to the window to see if Father had come back or if Ken had gotten a ride home from someone. As the afternoon wore on and it began to grow dark, Yuki grew more and more uneasy. She jumped when the telephone rang once more, but this time it was a call for the policemen informing them that they could leave their posts. They soon went off leaving only the FBI man to keep watch.

Yuki decided that the FBI had somehow found Ken and taken him off somewhere too, when at last he came home. Mother quickly took him to the kitchen, taking only a moment to introduce him to the FBI man. She wanted to explain things to him quietly and calmly so he wouldn't get upset or let his temper flare.

"And Dad still hasn't come back?" Ken asked when Mother told him of all that had happened.

Mother shook her head. "They didn't even tell us where they were taking him," she said, and for the first time she let her anxiety show.

"There were two policemen here too," Yuki added. "They wouldn't let anybody in to see us and they only left a while ago."

13

Ken looked troubled. "It's really serious then," he said soberly, and he got up to turn on the radio once more. "We heard some vague rumors at the library, but everybody just thought it was some fanatic doing something crazy. That's why I stayed to finish cramming for my exams."

Seeing the troubled expression on Ken's face, Yuki began to feel apprehensive. If this meant that the United States and Japan were at war, what was going to happen to them? Mother and Father were Issei (first-generation Japanese). They were as law-abiding and loyal as any American Yuki knew, but they had never been able to become citizens because of a law that wouldn't permit them to.

Ken seemed to be mulling over the same thought. He said something now about Mother and Dad becoming "enemy aliens" if this was really war.

"But that's silly," Yuki scoffed. "Just because they can't become citizens doesn't mean they're suddenly enemies now!"

Even as she spoke, however, she felt touched by a shadow of fear. What would the FBI do to Father if he was an "enemy alien"? Yuki wished he would hurry and come home.

The telephone shrilled into their anxious thoughts. The FBI man answered it, had a brief conversation, and then knocked on the kitchen door. "I've had orders to go back to headquarters," he explained. "I'll be leaving now."

"What about my father?" Ken asked. "When will he be released?"

The man shook his head. "I just don't know," he answered. "I really couldn't even hazard a guess."

Mother went to the door with him and bowed as she would to

any departing guest. The FBI man paused as though he wanted to say something friendly, but he didn't quite know what to say. "I hope everything will be all right for you," he said briefly, and then he was gone.

The house suddenly seemed empty and lonely, and Yuki flicked on the lights to scatter the gloom.

"Put the porch light on too, Yuki Chan," Mother reminded her. "Father may be back soon."

No one felt hungry, but Mother put supper on the table. Each time the telephone rang Mother or Ken hurried to answer it hoping it might be Father. But each time it was only an anxious friend.

"Mrs. Itoh says that Mr. Itoh was taken too," Mother explained after the last call. He was head of the Japanese Association in Oakland. It now became clear that the FBI was rounding up all the leaders of the Japanese community.

When Ken called his classmate, Jim Hirai, he discovered that Jim's father had been taken as well. Mr. Hirai was manager of one of the Japanese banks in San Francisco. "Looks like the FBI had a long list," Ken said dismally.

Now that the telephone was no longer monitored, it rang endlessly. Many of their Caucasian friends called to ask if they were all right. Mimi's mother phoned to ask if there was anything she could do. And Mrs. Jamieson called from across the street, becoming indignant and angry when she learned that Father had been taken by the FBI.

"Why he's the finest gentleman I know," she said firmly. "How dare they take him off like that?"

But they had indeed, and now it was almost eleven o'clock

15

and still he hadn't returned or even been permitted to call them. Mother forgot to remind Yuki about going to bed, so Yuki stayed up, blinking back the sleep that threatened, feeling tired and sad and empty inside.

Finally Mother spoke to her. "There's nothing you can do to help Father by staying up," she said. "Now run along to bed. Ken and I will wait up a little longer."

Yuki crept into her cold bed then, but discovered that she was no longer sleepy. She curled up into a small ball, trying to warm her icy feet, and felt the thumping of her heart. All around the night seemed dark and ominous and full of unfriendly sounds. A siren whined eerily down the street and Yuki wondered if it was the police rounding up more Japanese men. She could hear the foghorns droning drearily over the bay and felt glad to be safe in her own bed and not lost in some small boat floating in the foggy night. She heard the distant dull thud of an explosion and wondered if it could be a cannon. Had the war come to California? Suppose Japanese planes came to bomb San Francisco and Berkeley? Yuki shivered at the horrible thought and wiggled down deep in her bed. She heard the sound of a car slowing down near their house. Papa's back, she thought happily. Yuki leaped out of bed and ran barefooted into the living room to find Mother and Ken already at the door.

Mother turned away, disappointed. "It wasn't Papa San after all," she said. She left the screen door unlatched and checked the porch light once more.

"I can't sleep," Yuki said dismally.

Mother looked tired and worn. She still wore the apron she had put on to do the supper dishes and Yuki knew she had given no thought to going to bed.

16

"Well, let's all have some cake and hot chocolate then," she said. She was a believer in the solace of food and she seemed glad of something to do.

Ken's books were spread out over the dining room table, but he closed them and stacked them on his binder. "It's no use," he said. "I quit. Come on, Yuki, let's go have some food. Go put on your bathrobe and slippers."

Ordinarily, Yuki disliked being told what to do by her brother. "Just because you're bigger and older doesn't mean you can boss me around," she sometimes said to him.

If he was in a good mood, he'd laugh at her and tell her to get moving. But if he felt mean, sometimes he would just put a big hand at the back of her neck as though she were a basketball to be dribbled down the court and march her off to her room.

Ken was tall and strong, and he was the star forward on the Japanese Students Club basketball team. If he wanted to make Yuki march he could, whether she screamed or scratched or even tried to bite. Tonight he was strong, but there was a gentleness in his voice that made it seem all right for him to tell her what to do. It was the way Father spoke to her.

Everyone acknowledged the fact that Father was head of the house and listened with respect when he spoke. He had been in America four years longer than Mother, but he was proud of his heritage. He was the grandson of a Samurai and he behaved like one. He was brave and dignified and behind his strength was a gentle heart.

Mother still had many Japanese ways too. Every year on the third of March, she put out all her Japanese dolls for Dolls Festival Day, she put sweet cakes in front of Grandmother's photograph on her memorial day, and she still sat in the back seat of

17

the car instead of in front beside Father. She was a gentle Japanese lady, but she also had a strong and noble spirit.

Yuki was surprised at how hungry she was and remembered that she hadn't eaten very much supper. Her piece of chocolate cake disappeared even before Mother sat down and Yuki felt hungrier than ever.

"What else is there?" she asked. "I'm starved!"

Mother sliced some bread and got out some butter and homemade apricot jam. Ken said he felt like having some scrambled eggs and even offered to make them himself.

They felt a little better after they'd eaten, but they were all still worried about Father.

"I do hope he's had a good supper wherever he is," Mother said softly.

And then they lapsed into silence, for no one had any cheerful words to offer, and no one had the heart to voice the fears that were clamoring inside.

3
A
Lonely
Christmas

FOR five long days there was no word from Father. All during the day Mother waited for a phone call and each night she left the porch light on, but Father neither came home nor called. It was the same at Mrs. Itoh's house and at Jim Hirai's and at every other home where a father had been taken by the FBI. No one knew where the men were or even whether they were alive and well.

Mr. Toda called each day to ask if Father had returned, and one day he walked all the way to their house from the church dormitory in Oakland. He explained that he had done it for the exercise, but they knew that he was also trying to save the carfare.

He whispered to Mother when he thought Yuki wasn't listening. "It is rumored," he said ominously, "that the men were

19

taken as hostages; that they may be harmed if Japan kills any more Americans."

Yuki shuddered at the horror of the idea and was angry with Mr. Toda for even mentioning it. Mother was worried enough as it was. Yuki stalked out of the house, brushing past the old man without saying a word and whistling for Pepper. Pepper licked Yuki's face, wagging his tail and whimpering softly as though to console her. Even the big gray carp came swishing up to the surface of the pond, opening his mouth wide to make Yuki laugh. It was as though they knew the sadness and fear that troubled her and were trying to give her some cheer. Animals were really much nicer than people, Yuki thought. They never said things that could make you sad.

She thought now about red-haired Garvis who sat opposite her at school. The day after the Pearl Harbor attack he had leaned over and hissed, "You dirty Jap!"

Yuki was so angry she had shrieked back, "I am not! I'm not a Jap. I'm an American!" And she didn't care who heard her.

Miss Holt had stopped writing on the blackboard and had stated then and there to the entire class that the Japanese born in America, the Nisei, were just as American as anyone else in the school.

"They must never be confused with the Japanese militarists who attacked Pearl Harbor," she explained. "The Nisei are good and loyal citizens," she added emphatically, "just as you and I."

She brushed the chalk dust from her hands and looked straight at Garvis as she spoke. That made Yuki feel a little better, but she could never forget what he had said.

I hate you, Garvis Dickerson, she thought bitterly. It was a

good thing there were people like Mimi Nelson and Mrs. Jamieson to make up for the Garvises of the world. Mrs. Jamieson lived all alone and had a bad leg that gave her pain and heartache, but Yuki had never heard her say a cross or unkind word to anyone.

On the sixth day after he was taken away, a postcard finally arrived from Father. He told them that he was being held at the Immigration Detention Headquarters in San Francisco and asked for his shaving kit and some clean clothing.

"Am safe and well," he wrote, "and pray that you are too."

"Thank goodness," Mother sighed as she read it. It was not knowing where or how he was that had been the worst part of the long wait.

In a few more days, Father wrote that they could come to San Francisco to visit him and he hoped to see them soon. The very next day, Ken and Yuki stayed home from school and Ken drove them in the family car to San Francisco. Mother told him that while Father was away he was free to use the car as his own. Ken nodded absently. Any other time he would have been overjoyed to have the sole use of the car, but now there was little pleasure in the privilege. He drove silently over the Bay Bridge and scarcely spoke until they reached the Immigration Headquarters.

Yuki didn't like the looks of the building. Somehow all government buildings seemed austere and unfriendly, smelling of stale cigar smoke and cleaning fluids. She disliked this one more than most and hated the thought of Father being held there like a prisoner.

They waited for him in a small dark room, and when he came in followed by a guard, he looked tired and worn. Father, who never left the house without a neat crease in his trousers and a black bow tie at his neck, was tieless and rumpled, still wearing the gardening clothes in which he had been taken. He tried to be cheerful, however, and told them that everything was fine.

"Most of my friends are here," he explained. "There are over a hundred of us all sleeping on cots in one big room. It's like a college dormitory."

"Sounds more like jail than college," Ken said darkly, but Father ignored his remark.

"Are you getting enough to eat?" Mother asked anxiously. "And are you able to sleep?"

"What do you do all day, anyway?" Yuki asked.

Father answered all their questions patiently and asked many of his own. He wondered if they were getting along all right without him. "Do you have enough money? Have you been able to withdraw money from my account at the bank? Be sure to get the car lubricated this month, Kenichi," he reminded Ken.

It was only when their short visit was coming to an end that Father told them that he was among a group of ninety men being sent to an Army Internment Camp in Missoula, Montana.

"Montana!" Mother gasped.

"When do you leave?" Ken asked, trying to keep his voice steady.

"In a few hours," Father said. "I'm glad we had this chance to say goodbye."

Yuki was too stunned to say much. "But Montana is miles away," she said, her voice rising. "We won't be able to visit you."

Father nodded. "Not for a while, Yuki Chan, but I'll be back soon. Take good care of yourselves now, and Kenichi, look after your mother and sister for me. Be careful in every way."

23

Father hugged each of them silently and left the room quickly without turning back. Yuki tried to blink back the tears, but she couldn't keep them from streaming down her face.

"Oh, Mama," she squeaked, crying on her mother's shoulder just as she used to when she was a small child.

Mother held her close for a moment and then rose from her chair. She dabbed at her eyes, pulled on her gloves, and straightened her hat.

"Well, we mustn't just sit here the rest of the day," she said in a tight voice. "Come Yuki, Kenichi, let's go home and fix up a package to send to your father in time for Christmas."

Ken took Mother's arm and held it until they had reached the car. He helped Mother in and even gave Yuki a hand as she climbed in. Instead of making her feel better, however, Ken's gentleness only made Yuki sadder. Father was gone and Ken was trying hard to take his place, but they all knew he never could. And when would they ever see Father again?

It was a few days later that Ken made an announcement at suppertime. "I'm leaving school, Mom," he said matter-of-factly.

"Leaving the university?" Mother asked. "But why?"

"Most of my friends are leaving," Ken explained quickly. "The guys who live in Brawley and San Pedro and Los Angeles are all going back to help run the farms and businesses their fathers had to leave when they were interned. Besides," he added, his face suddenly growing stern, "everybody says there's going to be an evacuation."

"A what?" Yuki asked.

Ken looked at Mother, although it was Yuki who had asked

24

the question. "They say the government is going to move all the Japanese from the West Coast," he explained.

Yuki nearly choked on her lamb chop and Mother coughed into her tea.

"Don't be foolish, Kenichi," Mother scolded. "Why would the United States ever do a thing like that? We are not spies or traitors. And besides, you children are American citizens. You were born right here in California. How could they do anything like that to citizens?"

Ken shrugged. "There are a lot of people in California who'd be very happy to be rid of the Japanese competition in business and on the farms. They'd be glad to see us leave. It's people like that who spread those false rumors about sabotage in Hawaii when there wasn't any at all."

Ken's face was flushed and his voice was rising. He could get quite steamed up about anything that he thought was unfair or wrong.

Mother tried to quiet him. "People can get hysterical when they are afraid, Kenichi," she explained. "Fear sometimes makes people do terrible things."

"But why should we be victims of their stupid fears?" he asked bitterly.

Even Mother couldn't answer that. Ken thought that talk of an evacuation was more than a rumor, but Yuki couldn't believe him. How in the world could they ever gather up all the Japanese in California and shift them somewhere else? Where would they go? What would happen to all their homes? It was an impossible idea.

"You're crazy," she said to Ken.

25

But Ken said ominously. "You just wait. You'll see whether I'm crazy or not."

Christmas was bleak and drizzly, and not even the burning logs in the fireplace lent much cheer to the general gloom. There was no Christmas tree this year, for they decided it wouldn't be right to celebrate this wartime Christmas when men were fighting and dying in the Pacific and Father was interned in a Prisoner of War Camp in Montana.

Mother did bake her Christmas cookies as usual, however, and packed some in a red tin decorated with holly to send to Father. They packed nuts and candy and dried fruit as well, and put everything into a big carton along with some wool socks and caps and mittens for the thirty-below Montana winter that was engulfing Father and the other Japanese men with him.

Mother also packed tins of Christmas cookies for Mr. Toda and the minister's family at church, and for Mrs. Jamieson too. It was Yuki's task to deliver the cookies to the people at church on Sunday and on Christmas Eve to Mrs. Jamieson.

Yuki didn't like going to the parsonage at the back of the chapel because it was so dingy and always seemed to be in need of cleaning. The minister's three small children were usually underfoot and his wife, with her bulging eyes and scratchy voice, made Yuki feel uncomfortable. This time she was lucky, for no one was around. She put the cookies on the kitchen table beside the stack of unwashed dishes, glanced at the sink full of dirty pans, and left quickly. She hurried then to the dormitory building to look for Mr. Toda. He had a separate room and kitchen upstairs, but whenever Yuki had something for him she just hollered from the bottom of the dark narrow stairs and he came creaking down to get whatever she had.

"Thank you, Yuki Chan," he said bowing as he accepted the gift. "You are very kind."

"It was Mama who made the cookies," Yuki explained, wanting to give proper credit for Mother's efforts.

Mr. Toda nodded. "I know," he said, "but I thank you for bringing them to me." He was very proper, and careful to treat Yuki as a person and not just a child.

The tin Yuki liked most to deliver was the one for Mrs. Jamieson. Her house was warm and cozy and full of wonderful scents of dried rose petals and spices. She usually made a cup of hot cocoa for Yuki whenever she came to visit and then got out something from her bulging closet to show her. Sometimes it was her husband's stamp or shell collection. He had been the captain of a freighter and had collected stamps and shells from all over the world. Sometimes Mrs. Jamieson brought out her jewelry box full of precious stones and rings and bracelets and brooches that the captain had bought for her in Algiers or Istanbul or Lisbon. Yuki loved the jewelry box best.

"Golly, Mrs. Jamieson," she said when she first saw the jewels, "you're rich! You've got the jewels of a queen."

Mrs. Jamieson laughed the high lilting laugh that her parrot used to imitate. "My greatest wealth is in my friends, dear Yuki," she said. "Jewels are a cold comfort on a rainy winter's night."

On this Christmas Eve when Yuki appeared with her Christmas cookies, Mrs. Jamieson seemed sad and withdrawn. Yuki

27

could see that she hadn't even bothered to tint her flaming red hair that usually blossomed around her head like a flowering spring hat.

"Come in, come in," she said, and then without even waiting for Yuki to sit down, she gave her a small package. "Open it," she urged. "It's something I want you to keep to remember me by."

Yuki opened the gift quickly and discovered one of the pearl rings from Mrs. Jamieson's jewelry box.

"But Mrs. Jamieson," Yuki said astonished. "This is one of your best rings!"

"I know," Mrs. Jamieson said softly. "I want you to have it, so you won't ever forget me."

It was almost as though Mrs. Jamieson was trying to say goodbye.

"Why?" Yuki asked. "You aren't going away are you?"

Mrs. Jamieson shook her head. "No, no, I would never leave this house. But you people, Yuki . . . surely you've read the papers and heard the rumors. They say . . . well . . . it's terrible what they're saying."

"You mean about the evacuation?" Yuki said.

Mrs. Jamieson nodded. "It is a ghastly thought, but what are we to do? I've already sent off two letters to President Roosevelt, but I fancy he's not much inclined to listen to me."

So Mrs. Jamieson believed it would happen too, just as Ken did.

"Mother says they'd never do a thing like that," Yuki said gravely. "Besides, Ken and I are citizens."

"I know," Mrs. Jamieson said gently. "I wish that could make

28

a difference." Her voice trailed off into silence and there didn't seem to be much more to say. Yuki left her house feeling sad and puzzled. She held tightly the box with Mrs. Jamieson's pearl ring and wondered as she crossed the street whether it was indeed going to be a farewell gift.

By January there was no more doubt in anyone's mind. Even Mother no longer insisted that the evacuation was impossible, and her friends at church urged her to begin packing and clearing out their house.

On February 19, 1942, President Franklin D. Roosevelt issued an executive order authorizing the Secretary of War and his military commanders to prescribe areas from which any or all persons could be excluded.

"That means the entire West Coast," Ken said flatly, "and 'all persons' means us—the Japanese."

It was strange, Yuki thought, that the United States should be at war with Italy and Germany too, but that it was only the Japanese who were considered so dangerous to the country.

"It doesn't seem fair," she objected to Ken.

"The papers say it's for our own safety," Mother explained, trying to find some logical reason for such an illogical act.

Ken shrugged. "I'd rather take a chance and have the choice of being free," he said firmly.

"Me too," Yuki added.

But then, of course, no one had asked their opinion.

4
Ten Days
to
Pack

YUKI came home from school one day to find Mother sitting Japanese fashion on a cushion in the middle of her bedroom floor. She was surrounded by boxes and cartons containing old letters, notebooks, photographs, and papers that had been stored in her closet for years.

"What in the world are you doing?" Yuki asked.

Mother scarcely looked up. "I suppose I must throw them out," she said sadly. "They're old letters from your grandmother and uncle and aunts in Japan." She shuffled through some papers and held up some crayoned drawings. "Look, you did these in first grade," she explained. "And here are some by Kenichi. I just couldn't throw them out." There were boxes full of diaries too and assorted scraps of paper on which Mother had scribbled her thirty-one-syllable Japanese poems.

Yuki felt dizzy on Mother's behalf. "You'll never finish in time, Mama," she sighed. "What will you do?"

There was nothing Mother could do but keep sorting and tearing up and throwing out. "I'll just have to keep working until I finish," she said simply.

The evacuation hung over their heads now like the blade of the guillotine. No one knew just when it would take place, but everyone knew it was only a matter of time. One of these days the army would say, "Now," and they would have to be ready.

Already there was an eight P.M. curfew for all Japanese and they were forbidden to travel more than five miles from home. Shortwave radios, cameras, binoculars, and firearms were designated as contraband, and Ken had taken all their cameras, even Yuki's old box camera, and Dad's field glasses to the Berkeley police station.

Mother was anxious to observe every letter of the law. As soon as it was required that enemy aliens register, she had gone immediately to get registered. Ken too had registered at the Civil Control Station as head of their family. He had come home with a handful of baggage tags which were to be put on everything they would be taking into camp. "Look," he said, tossing the tags onto the table, "from now on we're family number 13453."

The house soon began to look as though a hurricane had swept through it. Mother sold the living room and dining room furniture by putting a "furniture for sale" sign up in the window. Ken rolled up the rugs and took down all the pictures on the walls. Decisions had to be made about everything in the house. What were they to do with the piano, the writing desk, Mother's sewing machine and cabinets, the beds and bureaus and chests,

Father's golf clubs, Yuki's doll collection, Ken's record player and all his records, the washing machine, the bedding, the china and silver and linens, the coffee table, the lamps. Yuki didn't know what poor Mother was going to do with it all. There seemed to be enough in their house to fill up all of Bekins Van and Storage and still have some left over.

Mother made dozens of lists and often misplaced half of them. She decided that all the large items would go into commercial storage. The rest of their belongings were spread around in the basements and attics and garages of various friends in Berkeley like orphaned children being distributed to concerned relatives. Their neighbors took as much as they could and the rest went to families they didn't even know, for members of some of the Berkeley churches had offered storage space in their homes to help the evacuating Japanese.

Yuki had her own small problems which seemed large enough at the time. She had to decide what to put into the trunks going to storage, what to throw out, and what to take with her into camp. Sometimes she would wake up in the middle of the night and suddenly decide to make changes, such as tucking Mrs. Jamieson's pearl ring safely into the storage trunk instead of into her camp suitcase.

"Remember," Ken cautioned, "we're only supposed to take whatever we can carry. That means no more than two suitcases each."

"OK," Yuki said, nodding, and every once in a while she would try lifting her two suitcases to see if she could carry them herself. But as she added to them day by day, they soon grew so heavy she could scarcely lift them off the floor. Eventually she

33

didn't even bother trying to lift them. Ken would simply have to help her.

Mother had an even bigger problem. Spread out in one corner of her room was an enormous canvas rucksack which she called the "going-to-camp-bundle." She had bought it for the blankets and bedding that they were required to take into camp with them, but gradually, she had begun to fill it with all sorts of odds and ends that wouldn't fit into her suitcases. Now it held the dishes and utensils they were also told to take to camp, as well as an electric hot plate, a kettle and tea pot, a can of tea, a hot water bottle, a thermos, two flashlights, rubber boots and umbrellas, and a small bed lamp. Already the bundle was beginning to bulge wildly in all directions, growing each day like some living creature.

Every once in a while Ken would look at it anxiously, saying, "I'll never make it into camp if I have to carry that enormous thing."

But Mother couldn't stop adding to it. "There is just no other place to put all the things we'll need," she said plaintively, and because Ken knew she was right, he watched in silence as the bundle grew bigger and bigger, dreading the day when he would have to stagger into camp with it.

After a while neither Ken nor Mother spoke of how they would manage getting the bundle into camp. It was something that would just have to happen.

There was another problem that none of them wanted to discuss, but one evening it was Mother who brought it up.

"We will have to find a home for Pepper soon," she said softly to Yuki. "You know we can't wait too much longer."

Yuki nodded. She knew something had to be done and very soon. Mimi couldn't take him because she already had a big German Shepherd and three guinea pigs. Mrs. Jamieson was taking Old Salt, but couldn't manage Pepper because of her lame leg.

"I'm not leaving Pepper with anybody I don't know," Yuki said firmly. "He'll be lonesome enough as it is."

The difficulty was, however, that most of their friends were going into camp with them, and if they weren't, they already had pets of their own. Mother looked troubled, but she knew how much Pepper meant to Yuki. "Well, perhaps a good idea will come to us soon," she said, and she put off the decision for another day.

Secretly, Yuki hoped both Mother and Ken would overlook the whole problem and then maybe she could simply pick Pepper up and carry him into camp as though it were the most natural thing in the world. Maybe in all the excitement no one would even notice.

More and more Ken was taking over as head of the house. Father signed the car over to him so it could be sold, and Ken was now able to withdraw money from Father's account. He made arrangements to buy War Bonds and signed up for Civil Defense.

Still that hadn't given him the right to do what he did, Yuki thought, for one day he made a decision about Pepper without even asking her. He simply said, "I found the perfect solution for Pepper. I put an ad in the Daily Cal at the university. Someone will want him and he'll be happy living with somebody my age. OK?"

"No, it's not OK," Yuki shouted angrily. "You didn't even ask me!"

35

"If I'd asked, you would have said no. Right?"

Yuki had to admit she most certainly would have.

"Well then," Ken went on, "what would be your solution?"

"I'm . . . well, I thought . . . I'm going to smuggle him into camp," Yuki said limply.

Ken didn't even give her solution a second thought. "It's settled then," he said quietly. "We'll make sure Pepper goes to a nice person. We'll all decide that together."

Ken did keep his word about that. Each time anyone came to see Pepper, he made sure that Yuki was there to meet him. Neither of them liked the first two boys who came. The first talked too much and the second one wanted Pepper for a fraternity house mascot. The third boy was a quiet sandy-haired sophomore named Andy. He had just lost his own dog and had been wanting another in its place.

"I live right here in Berkeley and could write you in camp to let you know how Pepper's doing," he said eagerly. His voice was gentle and Yuki saw how Pepper wagged his tail and licked his hand when Andy went to pet him.

"OK, Yuki?" Ken asked.

Yuki nodded. She gave Pepper one final hug and then ran into the house. She didn't want to stay and watch while Ken gave Andy Pepper's brush and comb and feeding dish. She hurried to her room and lay on her bed, holding her hands over her ears so she wouldn't hear Andy's car as it drove away with Pepper. Mother made her favorite barbecued spareribs for supper but Yuki could scarcely eat.

"I hate this whole stupid evacuation," she said grimly, and she ran outside, forgetting that there would be no Pepper to come

36

bounding up the steps to greet her. She went to the fishpond and threw pebbles into it, watching the old gray carp appear from beneath the lily pads, opening his mouth for something to eat. But tonight he didn't amuse her at all. Yuki stood there watching until it was too dark to see, biting her lip to keep back the tears.

As the house grew emptier, the garden seemed to grow more and more beautiful with spring flowers. The flowering cherry looked like a pale pink cloud and the peach trees blossomed like clusters of white popcorn.

In the midst of their frantic packing Yuki sometimes found Mother looking out the window and scribbling a poem on a scrap of paper. Yuki wished she could write poetry too. She was filled with indescribable feelings these days, but she couldn't find the right words to put them down on paper. It was like having an ache deep down inside, but not being able to tell anyone just where it was. Mother seldom spoke of her aches or sadness and rarely let anyone see her shed a tear, but she could make people understand how she felt by putting the right words in the fragile shell of poetry.

"You are truly a gifted and sensitive poet," Mr. Toda said admiringly. Mother scoffed, saying, "You are simply a biased and kind friend, Toda San." But Yuki knew that she was pleased.

Mother felt almost as strongly about her plants as Yuki had about Pepper. She couldn't bear to leave her favorite plants for strangers who would come after they left. She dug up her London Smoke carnation, the yellow calla lilies, and the Berkshire climbing rose and gave them to Mrs. Jamieson and Mrs. Nelson. A few of Father's prize *bonsai* went to the minister of the Congregational Church. "I'll take good care of them and return them whenever you come back," he promised.

Some of Father's best gladiolas, however, went to a woman from up the block whom they scarcely knew. She appeared one day with a carton and trowel and asked if she could have them. "I thought you wouldn't mind," she explained, "since you're leaving anyway."

Yuki didn't want her to have them, but Mother said it didn't matter. "Let her have them if they will make her happy," she said.

Ken called her a vulture. "She's as bad as the people in San Pedro who are buying refrigerators for five dollars and cars for twenty-five dollars from the Japanese who have to go first," he said bitterly.

On April 21, 1942, the headline in the Berkeley paper read, JAPS GIVEN EVACUATION ORDERS HERE. Yuki shivered as she read it. "I wish they'd stop calling us Japs," she murmured. But that was the least of her problems now. The army had finally issued the order that said all the Japanese in Berkeley must evacuate their homes. They were to report to the Tanforan Assembly Center by noon on May 1st.

"That gives us exactly ten days," Ken said nervously. "Think we can make it, Mom?"

"We'll have to make it, Kenichi," Mother said calmly.

Then she poured his coffee and Yuki's hot chocolate. "Eat your breakfast now," she said to them. "Evacuation orders or not, we still have to eat."

39

5
Inside
the
Barbed
Wire

IT was their last day in the house where Yuki had spent all her life until now. The furniture was gone, the cupboards and shelves were empty, and all that remained were three mattresses on the floor where they would sleep one more night. In the morning the blankets would be put into their "going-to-camp" bundle and Mrs. Nelson would see that the Salvation Army picked up the old mattresses.

Yuki could hear Mother's footsteps echoing in the empty house as she went from room to room sweeping out the floors and making a last check.

"What difference does it make whether the house is clean now?" Yuki asked, puzzled.

But Mother was neat and conscientious to the very end. "Of

41

course it matters," she said. "I want to leave a nice clean house for whoever will rent it after we're gone."

"What we should've done is bought this house," Yuki said slowly. She hated the idea of anyone else living in it. It was their house and nobody else belonged in it. The owner, Mr. Rudolphson, had said as much. "It won't be the same, Mrs. Sakane," he had said sadly. "I hate to see you go."

Mother reminded Yuki, however, that the people who owned their homes had the problem of finding someone suitable to rent and maintain their houses while they were gone. Whether one owned or rented, it was a difficult time for anyone who was Japanese.

Mimi's mother invited them to dinner on their last night. She made roast turkey with all the trimmings, as though it were Thanksgiving or Christmas. And for dessert she baked two different kinds of pie so Ken could have a piece of each. "Just in case you don't get any homemade pie for a while," she explained.

Mr. Nelson reminded them again and again that they were to write if there was anything he could do for them while they were in camp.

"Me too," Mimi added eagerly. "Write me if you want anything." Then she hurried to her room and brought presents for each of them. There was a box of initialed white linen handkerchiefs for Mother, a lei of Lifesavers for Ken, and for Yuki a red leather diary wrapped in pink tissue and ribbon. "So you can put down everything that happens to you and write me about it," she told Yuki.

It was a pleasant evening, and for a while Yuki almost forgot why they were having dinner at Mimi's at all. When they got home, Mrs. Jamieson came to say goodbye in case she missed them in the morning.

"My, we can't even offer you a chair," Mother said, looking around at the emptiness that surrounded them. "Not even a cup of tea."

Mrs. Jamieson waved away Mother's concern and fumbled inside the small beaded bag she carried on her arm. She pulled out a small white envelope and pressed it into Mother's hand. "This may come in handy someday," she whispered. "Or, if you can, get something nice for the children."

She promised to take good care of Old Salt, and then with a quick hug, smelling of lavender and spices, for each of them, she was gone. When Mother opened the envelope she found a crisp twenty dollar bill.

Yuki woke up the next morning feeling the blankets being pulled off her. "Hey," she shouted, trying to hold on to them. But Ken quickly deprived her of their warmth and stuffed them into the big rucksack.

"Get going, Yuki," he warned. "We have to be at the Civil Control Station in just one hour."

Yuki shivered without her blankets, but she wanted to stay curled up on her own mattress on her own floor in her own room for as long as possible. She didn't leap up until she heard the front doorbell and Mrs. Nelson's cheerful voice as she brought over a tray of coffee and hot chocolate and sweet rolls oozing with butter.

When Mrs. Nelson came back later with Mimi, it was to drive them to the church designated as the Civil Control Station where all the Japanese were to report.

43

Mimi squeezed Yuki's hand. "Are you ready?" she asked.

"I guess so," Yuki said lamely. But she didn't really know what she was ready for. All her belongings were gone and her room was empty, but whether she was ready for what lay ahead, Yuki didn't know. She felt numb and strange, as though she were inside somebody else's body.

Mr. Nelson helped Ken secure ropes around their big camp bundle and squeeze it into the trunk of the car. They put the baggage on the floor between their feet and carried smaller bundles on their laps. There was no room for Mr. Nelson to come with them, and he stayed behind, waving until their car turned the corner. Yuki tried to smile as she waved, but she couldn't make her mouth do as she wished. In fact, she wasn't sure whether she had control of her stomach either, and for a few tense minutes she was afraid she might lose her breakfast. She felt pale and green and when she glanced at Mother, she noticed that the color was gone from her face as well.

The grounds of the Congregational Church were crowded with people and baggage and armed soldiers. Hundreds of Japanese had gathered from all parts of the city, looking like refugees with their odd-shaped bundles and assorted belongings. There were children running around, and others were crying. There were deputies telling people what to do with their baggage, and much to Ken's relief there were dozens of big trucks into which all the baggage was being loaded.

"Whew," he said, grinning for the first time that morning. "I won't have to carry that rucksack into camp after all."

"They should've told you there'd be trucks," Mimi said indignantly.

"I'll say," Yuki agreed. "I would've brought lots more things if I'd known."

"That's exactly why they didn't tell us about the trucks," Mother said knowingly.

But now the Nelsons were being directed to unload their passengers quickly and move on. There was a mad jumble of hugs and kisses.

"Be careful now. Don't forget to write and send me your address," Mimi called.

"I will . . . I won't . . . I will . . ." Yuki scarcely knew what she was saying or doing. She was being hugged. Mother was bowing. Ken was shaking hands. And then they were making their way into the big assembly hall, passing the soldiers who stood at each doorway with bayonets mounted and ready.

Inside there were hundreds of Japanese people, and the low rumble of their voices filled the large hall as they exchanged greetings and rumors. Old people were sitting quietly, looking patient and resigned. Mothers were comforting crying infants, youngsters were shrieking and running about, young people were greeting their friends, and through all the commotion the women of the church moved in and out serving sandwiches and coffee and milk. No one felt like eating, however, and the sandwich trays remained mostly untouched.

The minister of the church was going from group to group, shaking hands, greeting those he knew and comforting those who looked bewildered and frightened. Ken found some of his classmates and went over to talk to them, laughing and joking to cover up what he really felt. Mother sat quietly on one of the folding chairs and Yuki went to sit beside her. She wished Father were here. Surely he would have found some way to comfort Mother, to take away the bleak look on her face. Yuki felt scared, but there was also the strange excitement of plunging into a new adventure. She had just found some of her own classmates and went to talk to them when it was time to line up and board the buses.

The buses, like giant vacuum cleaners, were sweeping up all the Japanese from the streets of the city. As Yuki waited to get into one, she noticed large groups of people gathered across the street to watch. She wondered what they were thinking. Were they relieved to see the Japanese go? Were they glad to be rid of them? Some of them chatted gaily, some looked grim, and some simply stared blankly.

The buses sped quickly down familiar streets, past the high school, past the little Japanese food store, its windows now boarded up, past the markets where they often went food shopping, and then down the approach toward the Bay Bridge. Instead of going to San Francisco, however, the buses continued down the Bayshore Highway, taking the same route Father followed when he drove visitors from Japan to Stanford University to see the chapel and campus. Today, however, everything on the highway seemed different. Maybe it was because she felt so different inside, Yuki thought. Maybe because she wasn't Yuki Sakane today, but simply a number sitting on a special bus.

It wasn't long before Ken pointed to the grandstand of Tanforan Racetrack looming on the left of the highway. Yuki could see the barbed-wire fence that encircled the entire area and the tall watchtowers that pierced the fence at regular intervals. The buses turned in toward the racetrack and moved quickly between the armed guards who stood at the gates.

"Well, here we are at the Tanforan Assembly Center," Ken said dryly. It was one of fifteen such centers that had been rushed into completion on fair grounds and racetracks to house the 110,000 Japanese who had been evacuated from the West Coast of the United States.

The buses moved slowly toward the grandstand area, and as Yuki turned to look back at the gates, she saw the armed guards swinging them shut. There was no turning back now; they were locked inside.

6
Home Is a Horse Stall

CROWDED along the rail around the racetrack, watching for arriving friends, were hundreds of Japanese who had been evacuated earlier from the Bay Area. The first familiar face Yuki saw was Mr. Toda. She waved eagerly and he waved back in an awkward sort of salute. Yuki waved again and again, feeling better just at the sight of someone she knew.

As they got off the bus, they were directed to an area roped off beneath the grandstand where each family registered, filled out forms, and went through a brief medical inspection. The baggage they carried was inspected for contraband and then they were assigned living quarters.

"Barrack 16, Apartment 40," Ken read from the slip handed to him.

"Golly," Yuki said impressed, "we get an apartment!" She

49

had never lived in an apartment and found the prospect intriguing. She moved eagerly now, keeping close to Ken.

"Hey, Ken!" It was Ken's classmate Jim Hirai.

"Hey, Jim!" Ken shouted back, and they pounded each other on the back as though they hadn't seen each other for ten years.

"I'll help you find your quarters," Jim offered.

But now Mother was surrounded by her church friends who had arrived two days earlier. She was bowing and greeting them as though they were meeting on the sunny walk outside their church in Oakland. They quickly exchanged barrack numbers and Mr. Toda and the minister promised to come visit them later.

"I am in the Bachelors' Quarters here," Mr. Toda said rather dismally. "I must share a room with five other men. It is a strange new life," he added, and he did not look happy.

Yuki was anxious to see where they would be living. "Come on, Mama," she urged, and they quickly followed Ken and Jim down the racetrack.

It had rained the night before and the track was muddy and pocked with puddles. Yuki's new saddle shoes were soon covered with mud and Mother's blue kid shoes were oozing with it. "I'm glad I packed rubber boots for us," she remarked, and she held on to Yuki's arm to keep from slipping.

As they walked along, Yuki saw that wherever there was room tar-papered army barracks had been put up for the eight thousand Japanese who would soon be living there. Barrack 16, however, was not among them. Now Ken and Jim were leaving the northern end of the track and disappearing beyond a cluster of eucalyptus trees. When Yuki and Mother caught up with them, they were going up the wide ramp of a stable that stood about a foot above the ground. There was a sign tacked to a corner of the stable that read "Barrack 16."

"This isn't a barrack at all," Yuki said, disappointed. "It's just a dirty old stable."

They followed Ken and Jim along the narrow walk that took them past a dozen stalls, each marked with a number, and then stopped in front of the one marked "40."

"Well, this is it," Jim said, nudging the door open.

The stall was narrow and dark, with two small windows high up on either side of the door. It measured about ten by twenty feet and was empty except for three army cots that lay folded on the floor. There were no mattresses or bedding of any kind. Dust and dirt and woodshavings still littered the linoleum that had been hastily laid over the manure-covered floor, and Ken sniffed at the lingering odor left by the former occupants.

"Boy," he said wrinkling his nose. "There's no mistaking who lived here before us."

Yuki looked around the stall feeling as though she'd been handed an empty ice cream cone. "This is an apartment?" she asked, dismayed.

"That, my dear child, is what is known as a euphemism," Jim said to her. "You'll get used to things like that here."

Yuki didn't know what Jim meant, but she didn't want to show her ignorance. She grinned at him and went to inspect the rear half of the stall which was separated from the front by a dutch door worn down with teeth marks. The walls had been whitewashed so hurriedly that insects hadn't had time to escape, and their small white corpses still clung to the walls along with cobwebs and horseshoes and rusty nails.

Even Mother, who usually found something cheerful to say about most difficulties, seemed at a loss for words. "Well," she said at last, "the first thing we need to do is sweep out this place. Can you help us find a broom, Jim?"

In the two days he had been in camp, Jim had quickly learned where to find things. "Sure," he said, "and you'll need some mattresses too. Come on, Ken, let's go."

The boys set up the cots before they left, putting up two in the inner half of the stall for Yuki and Mother and one up in front for Ken. Yuki blew off the dust from the springs and Mother brushed away what she could with her handkerchief. Then she sat down, took off her hat and gloves and put them down on the cot beside her.

"Oh, Mama," Yuki said, laughing, "you sure didn't need a hat and gloves to come live in a horse stall!"

Mother never went anywhere without a hat and gloves, not even to the corner to mail a letter. It was a habit she had acquired when she first arrived in America, and she had never changed since. She was a perfect lady, and Yuki supposed she always would be.

She smiled now at Yuki and brushed the dust from her hands. "You're right, Yuki Chan," she said, wistfully. "I guess I will hardly be needing a hat when I go out here."

Everyone who had been at Tanforan for more than a day seemed to be dressed in slacks and sweaters, wearing a bandana because of the dust and wind. Mother didn't even own a pair of slacks, and Yuki had never seen her put anything but a hat on her head.

"I'll lend you one of my scarves," she offered, and then she left Mother to rest on the cot and went out to investigate the surrounding area.

The latrines and washroom for their section were about a hundred feet away, and when Yuki saw those, she knew that Mother would have much more to worry about than not having slacks or a scarf. None of the toilet cubicles had doors and neither did the showers. There were no wash basins, but only a long tin trough that seemed more appropriate for horses.

Yuki hurried back to their stall and shouted as she burst inside. "Golly, Mama, you should see the latrines!" She stopped when she saw Jim. "Oh," she murmured, embarrassed.

But Jim just kept right on sweeping and Ken said, "That's OK, Yuki. We know what they're like. No doors." Apparently Jim had already told Ken all about the inadequacies of camp life.

Yuki flopped down on one of the cots and bounced tentatively on the mattress the boys had just brought back. It rustled noisily and scratched her legs.

"It's stuffed with straw!" she shouted. "This must've been left over from the horses."

But Jim quickly told her she was lucky to have any mattress at all. "We got the last three they had," he explained.

"*Mah,*" Mother sighed. Already she was worried for the people who would come later and discover that there were no mattresses for them.

53

As Yuki sat squirming on the prickly straw mattress, she suddenly realized that she was famished. "No wonder," she mused aloud. "We didn't have any lunch."

"That's right," Ken said wearily. "I thought I was beginning to grow weak." It was probably the first time in Ken's life that he'd gone for more than four hours without food of some kind.

"Well, supper's at five o'clock and you'd better get to the mess hall early," Jim warned them. "The lines are long and it takes forever to get inside." Then, glancing at his watch he hurried to his own quarters to take a shower before supper.

By the time Yuki, Ken, and Mother got to the mess hall in the grandstand, people were streaming toward it from all parts of the hundred-acre camp. Already several long lines had formed and those who had received their baggage were holding the plates and utensils they'd been instructed to bring. They stood silently and patiently, waiting for the lines to move.

The sun was going down now and the wind whipped through the open stretches of the racetrack sending swirls of dust in everyone's face. Yuki shivered and turned her back to the wind, huddling close to Mother to try to keep warm.

It was almost an hour before they got inside the gloomy mess hall and to the serving table. A white-aproned man was using his fingers to put two canned sausages on each person's plate from a dishpan piled high with sausages. Another man gave each of them one boiled potato and a piece of bread.

"Is this all?" Ken asked.

The men nodded silently. At home Ken would have considered this only an appetizer.

The enormous room was filled with wooden picnic tables, but with five thousand people milling about, it was hard to find a vacant table. At last they found one they could share with an old man and a young family with two crying babies. When they sat down, however, Yuki no longer felt like eating. The sight of the sausages heaped high in the dishpan hadn't helped. Mother must have felt the same, for Yuki saw her quietly slip her sausages on Ken's plate and take only a few bites of her potato.

They left as soon as Ken finished eating, walking carefully along the dark muddy track. Tanforan wasn't equipped for nighttime use and there were few lights to help them find their way.

Their small stall now looked more bleak than ever, and the single electric bulb that dangled from the ceiling made only a forlorn effort to brighten the darkness. Their stall faced north and the cold wind that blew in from the crevices around the windows and door made the light bulb sway and cast eerie shadows on the wall.

Yuki pulled her coat tightly around her and sat hunched on Ken's cot. "I'm beginning to hate this place already," she murmured.

"You know what I'd like right now?" Ken asked dreamily. "A nice juicy steak, medium rare, with onions on the side and a big baked potato full of sour cream, and a huge piece of apple pie with ice cream and . . ."

"Stop it!" Yuki shrieked. "You're giving me hunger pangs."

Mother opened her purse and felt in all its corners. "I don't even have any candy," she said dismally. It was a sad day for Mother when she couldn't offer something good to eat to provide her family some comfort. She looked helpless and frail as she glanced around the stall, unable to find anything in it that would offer some cheer.

"If only our baggage would come," she said. "I could at least make some hot tea."

And then as though her thoughts had miraculously produced the fact itself, they heard a truck pull up outside the stable.

"Hey, Sakane family," a voice shouted. "Does this monster belong to you?"

It was their camp bundle. Ken rushed to the door to claim it even though he was embarrassed to admit it. "Right here," he called out.

As soon as he had wedged the big bundle through the narrow door, Ken untied the ropes and they quickly pulled out all the things Mother had packed inside. Every familiar and useful object looked like an old friend. Yuki ran to the washroom to fill the kettle with water, Ken hooked up the hot plate and Mother began putting the blankets and sheets on the cots.

Yuki sat close to the hot plate, watching its coils glow with heat and feeling better as the water in the kettle began to hum.

She jumped when she heard a knock at the door. It was Mr. Toda, shivering without a coat in the brisk night air. "I've brought you a little something," he said to Yuki, holding out a small bag of peanuts.

Yuki couldn't have been happier if it were a sack of gold. "Oh, Mr. Toda," she squealed. "You're wonderful!" And she gave the surprised old man a hug that embarrassed him.

"It is only one bag of peanuts," he said sheepishly.

Yuki divided it carefully, pouring a few into each of their palms. Ken popped his handful into his mouth and swallowed the whole thing down in one delicious gulp, but Yuki ate one peanut at a time, chewing carefully and slowly, savoring each small bite.

56

Mother was happy now, making tea and serving it in the cups she had packed. "Well, here we are," she said, smiling at Mr. Toda, "having tea together just as we used to at home."

"Ha," Mr. Toda answered with a sad half-smile. "It is hardly like being in your home, Mrs. Sakane."

And even as he spoke, they could hear the voices of the people who lived all around them, for the walls between each stall lacked a foot from the ceiling, and every sound except for the smallest whisper traveled easily to the next stall.

No fighting with Ken here, Yuki thought, listening. No secrets at all. And she popped the last peanut into her mouth, recalling with sudden longing Mrs. Nelson's delicious turkey dinner.

7
A New Friend

UKI awoke to the sound of hammering and pulled the blanket up over her head to keep out the noise. For a moment she thought she was back in Berkeley, but as she moved, the noisy rustle of straw reminded her where she was. It was dark and Yuki thought it must still be about six o'clock. She flopped over and tried to find her way back to sleep, but the hammering began again.

"Stop it, Ken," she shouted toward the front of the stall. "You're going to wake everybody up with all that noise."

The hammering stopped and then after a brief silence a voice apologized for waking her up. Yuki was wide awake now, for it wasn't Ken who had answered her. It was their neighbor from the other side of the partition that divided their stalls. Now Yuki heard the voice of a young girl whisper, "How can anybody still be asleep at nine o'clock?"

Yuki flushed with embarrassment. "I'm sorry," she murmured. "I thought it was my brother."

She leaped from her cot and saw that Mother's cot was already empty. So was Ken's. She had slept right through breakfast, but Mother had brought back some toast for her and left a note saying she'd gone to do some laundry. By the time Yuki came back from washing her face, however, Mother had already returned with her laundry still unwashed.

"Imagine," she said wearily. "All the tubs were already taken and there were at least six people waiting for every tub. Besides that the hot water had run out."

"No hot water already?" It was a woman's voice from the next stall. She had joined in their conversation as though she were sitting right there beside Yuki.

"They say there might be more this afternoon," Mother called back. "But no one seems to know when."

"Ah well," the woman answered, "I really don't want to do a wash anyway and I cannot abide those terrible showers. I nearly scalded myself yesterday!"

The voice was that of an older woman. Yuki pictured her as being small and gray-haired, with gold-rimmed glasses sliding halfway down her nose. "I'm going to have a good soak," she went on, "even if I have to find an old barrel."

"Oh, Grandma!" It was the young girl again.

Yuki simply had to see what her neighbors looked like. She burst out of the door and at almost the same moment, a young girl about Yuki's age opened the neighbor's door. Her straight black hair was pulled back into two long braids and her small thin face was intense and serious.

60

"Hi!" Yuki said.

The girl looked her up and down and said softly, "Hello. My grandfather says he's sorry he woke you up."

"Oh that's OK," Yuki said quickly. "I'm sorry I yelled at him. Are you living with your grandparents then?"

The girl nodded. "My parents are dead," she said simply.

Yuki scarcely knew what to say in response to a statement of such finality. So far in her life, Yuki had not met death or even brushed close to it, except for the time her first dog had died. Even then, she hadn't seen a dead being. She had only left a sick dog at the veterinarian's and never seen him again. She couldn't even begin to conceive of the sadness of living without her mother and father. She searched for a way, somehow, to share in the girl's grief and said, "My father's interned. He's been taken to Montana."

The girl's grandmother peered out of their stall now and motioned to both of them. "Invite your friend inside, Emiko," she said.

The old woman didn't look at all the way Yuki had imagined. She was short and plump, with great rolls of flesh around her stomach and a broad smile that revealed a missing tooth at each side of her mouth. It seemed strange to see a woman her age wearing slacks, but she seemed perfectly at ease in them.

"Come in, come in," she urged once more.

Their stall was just like the one Yuki lived in, but it was a mad jumble of cots, baggage, cartons, and boxes. It was obvious they had brought a great deal more than they could carry by hand.

Emiko's grandfather was in the rear of the stall taking apart

61

some wooden crates and rebuilding them into a rough but sturdy table. No wonder he was making such a racket, Yuki thought. He scarcely looked up as she came in, but nodded as he hammered to indicate that he had taken note of her presence.

"Grandfather," the old woman called to him. "This is our neighbor." And then she quickly learned Yuki's name and all about her family.

"Our name is Kurihara," the old woman said, "but you can just call me Grandma. We had a Japanese food shop in San Francisco where we sold bean curd cake and fresh tuna and rice and tins of bamboo shoot and eel and . . ."

Yuki swallowed hard. "You're making me hungry," she admitted. "I've been starved since yesterday."

Emiko's grandmother stopped in dismay. "Hungry!" she exclaimed. "Why, wait a minute then." And plugging in her electric hot plate, she set a small wire screen on it and put five rice cakes filled with sweet bean paste on top to toast. "I brought these along from our shop," she said, smiling at her own cleverness. "They're a little stale, but they'll be fine in a minute."

The old woman swept aside some clothing to make space on a box for Yuki to sit down and then, like Mother, quickly got out her teapot to make tea for her new visitor. She glanced at her granddaughter as she bustled about.

"Talk to your new friend, Emiko," she urged. Then turning to Yuki she explained, "She's not a very talkative one, but you will become friends." She announced the last as though she were in charge of the world and had decided that it would be so.

Yuki didn't mind at all. It would be wonderful to have a

friend next door. They wouldn't even need a telephone to talk to each other. All they'd have to do was call out over the partition.

When the cakes were properly toasted, Mrs. Kurihara poured some tea and called to Mother to come join them. There was much bowing and greeting when Mother came in and Emiko's grandfather even put down his hammer and came to have tea with them.

Yuki never cared much for Japanese sweet cakes. She would far rather have had a piece of chocolate cake or a hot buttered Danish pastry, but this was a strange new life and eating Japanese cakes in the middle of the morning seemed to be a part of it.

"Imagine serving tea to a guest for the first time in a horse stall," Emiko's grandfather said, shaking his head. "I never dreamed that America would do such a thing to us."

But Mrs. Kurihara refused to share the old man's dejection. "Well, if we had not been sent here, we never would have met Mrs. Sakane or Yuki. So there is something to be happy about after all, isn't there?" And she laughed a hearty laugh that gave her plump body a good shake, and Yuki couldn't help but laugh with her.

Ken was gone all morning, and when he got back, he had several pieces of used lumber and a pocketful of nails. He looked as pleased as though he'd found some sunken treasure.

"I got all this at the discarded lumber pile," he said with a pleased grin. "Jim's coming over this afternoon to help me put up some shelves."

"How about making us a table too," Yuki suggested.

"And a bench would be nice," Mother added.

"In that case I'd better go back and get more lumber," Ken said quickly. "It's disappearing like snow on a hot day."

"Let me come with you then." It was Emiko's grandfather, and now it was Ken's turn to discover that their lives had become hopelessly entangled with their neighbors' whether they liked it or not.

The neighbors on the other side were a quiet elderly couple whose children had married and gone away. The man had been a barber and offered to cut Ken's hair for him whenever he wanted a haircut. They were pleasant neighbors and kept pretty much to themselves.

By afternoon Yuki began to feel bored. "Let's go scout around the rest of the camp, Emi," she suggested to her new friend. "Let's go see if the other stables are any better."

They set off quickly, circling the wide track and going in the opposite direction from the grandstand. They discovered that there were dozens of stables like theirs. They were called "converted buildings," another euphemism, as Jim would say. And whenever they ran into friends, they discovered that the complaints were the same everywhere. The latrines were dirty and doorless, there wasn't enough toilet paper, the showers couldn't be adjusted properly, and the food was horrible.

"It's the same all over," Yuki observed. "The whole camp is pretty awful."

They eventually found the Bachelors' Quarters and Yuki discovered Mr. Toda sitting outside in the sun playing *Go* with a bald-headed man. They were discussing the war as they pondered their moves.

"Perhaps Japan will win," the bald-headed man said. "Look what they did to Pearl Harbor."

Yuki was shocked to hear such talk. None of her parents' friends had such silly notions. "She is *not* going to win," Yuki said hotly. "America will win because we're fighting for what's right."

The old man glanced up from the *Go* board and blinked as he looked at her. "Ha, you are young and do not know very much."

Yuki was ready to explode when Mr. Toda came to her defense. "I do not agree with you, old man," he said firmly. "I believe she is right." And then he put one of his black stones in just the right place to win the game.

"Good," Yuki said, pleased. "You've won."

She didn't like the bald-headed, sour-voiced old man and wanted to get away from him quickly. "C'mon Emi, let's go," she urged and with a quick goodbye to Mr. Toda, she and Emi hurried on to finish their tour of the camp.

It was too bad Mr. Toda had to live with a man like that, Yuki thought. She hoped there weren't any more like him in camp. That was the whole trouble with scooping up all the Japanese like so many fish in a net and dumping them into one big camp. The good were thrown in with the bad, the kind with the mean, the gentle and polite with the selfish and greedy. It was just sheer luck that they had been squeezed in between two pleasant neighbors.

Yuki turned to Emi and said, "I sure am glad you live next door."

Emi nodded. "Me too—about you," she said with a quick grin, and Yuki felt much better.

65

8
Ken
Spoils a
Party

As soon as Yuki heard, she ran home to tell Emi. "There's going to be a wedding at the church this afternoon!" she shouted breathlessly.

Emi didn't have to be told any more. "When shall we go?" she asked.

The days were beginning to grow long and dull, and until the schools opened Yuki and Emi were constantly watching for any unusual event, outside of going to the recreation hall, that would add some excitement to their day.

Yuki and Emi went to the church barrack early and stood outside waiting to catch a glimpse of the bride. Inside they could hear a small reed organ pumping out the wedding march, and then they saw the bride. She was smiling and radiant, wearing a white satin gown and carrying a bouquet of white roses ordered from outside. Friends of the couple had gotten some rice to

67

throw at them, and Yuki picked up whatever she could from the ground and tossed a few grains herself. Then the couple climbed into a car decorated with signs and tin cans and drove off amid shouts and laughter and the honking of horns.

"Where will they go?" Emi wondered. "They can't leave camp, can they?"

"Let's find out," Yuki suggested and they took off, running as fast as they could to keep the car in sight. It headed toward the grandstand and then went around and around the track several times before it finally drove off toward one of the stables where the newlyweds would make their home.

Yuki groaned. "What a honeymoon that was!" she said dismally.

"I'll say," Emi agreed. "Maybe they'll have a party later on with wedding cake."

"And ice cream," Yuki added. "With sandwiches and nuts."

"Uh-huh. And hamburgers."

"And steaks and french fries with catsup."

"Oh, they don't serve things like that at a wedding party," Emi said at last.

"I know it," Yuki said sighing. "It just felt good to think about those things."

It seemed they were always thinking about food. In fact, Yuki had just written to Mimi asking her to please send something good to eat. "I'm up to my ears in potatoes and bread and weenies and beans," she complained shamelessly. "I'd give a million dollars for a milk shake and a hamburger!"

Mimi and her mother not only sent in a package of cookies and crackers and cheese, but as soon as visitors were permitted to come, they drove down with Mrs. Jamieson, laden with good things to eat and flowers from their garden.

When the messenger arrived with a notice telling them that they had visitors, Yuki ran all the way to the grandstand. Visitors were not permitted onto the camp grounds and had to be met during visiting hours in the grandstand hall. The large room was crowded with visitors from outside, but Yuki quickly spotted Mimi's red dress and her long blond hair. Mrs. Nelson stood beside her, laden with packages, and next to her sat Mrs. Jamieson, her flame-colored hair tinted beautifully, holding a large box carefully in her lap.

"Mimi!" Yuki shouted joyfully. "Mrs. Nelson! Mrs. Jamieson!"

It was a great laughing, hugging, hand-shaking reunion and everyone wanted to talk at once. "We had to wait in line for two hours before they let us in," Mimi said ruefully.

"I know," Yuki nodded sympathetically. "We stand in line for everything inside the fence too. It's a lousy system."

"I baked a chocolate cake for you, Yuki," Mrs. Jamieson said, thrusting the big package toward her. "It's got chopped walnuts and marshmallows in the frosting."

"And here are more crackers and cheese and nuts and cookies," Mrs. Nelson added, setting off another round of hugs and squeals and much bowing by Mother.

If only Ken were here to help them carry everything back to their stable, Yuki thought, but Ken was busy working as an orderly at the hospital where he earned eight dollars a month. If he ever got promoted he would earn twelve dollars a month.

"Some salary," he had laughed, but even the top professionals

69

made only sixteen dollars a month, so Ken could scarcely complain. That was the established rate for all the evacuees and no one could earn more.

As Yuki looked around the big hall, she suddenly saw Ken at the other end of the room. He was with several of his college classmates talking to some Caucasian men and women. They seemed to be listening intently to whatever it was the visitors were saying and it must have been important enough for Ken to take time off from work.

"There's Ken," Yuki said. "I'll go get him."

But first she had to know about Old Salt and about Pepper. Mrs. Nelson had called Andy just before they came. Then Yuki and Mother described their stable, the smaller mess halls that had now opened throughout camp, the churches, the hospital, the library, and the recreation centers, and by the time Yuki turned to look for Ken, he and his visitors were gone.

It was soon time for all visitors to leave and the kisses and hugs were not as joyful. "We'll be back soon," Mrs. Nelson promised.

"With more cake and cookies," Mrs. Jamieson added. She squeezed Yuki's hand and said, "You know, not a day goes by that we don't think about you."

"Me too," Yuki said. And it was true. As full as her mind was of her new friends and her new life, she always thought of their old house and the neighbors and Pepper and Old Salt after she got in bed and closed her eyes. And whenever she dreamed, it was always of their old home back in Berkeley, never about camp. It seemed that half of her was still back home even though her physical self was sitting in a horse stall in Tanforan.

"See you soon, Yuki," Mimi called, and she turned to wave again and again until she disappeared through the door.

That evening as they lined up outside the mess hall for supper, Yuki asked Ken, "Who were you talking to during visiting hours? You missed Mimi and her mother and Mrs. Jamieson."

Ken seemed distracted and absently swung the container with their dishes inside.

"Be careful, Kenichi, the dishes will break," Mother warned. But Ken's mind was on other things.

"Huh?" Yuki asked again. "Who were those people?"

"From the university," Ken replied at last. "One was the Dean of Men and one was the Executive Secretary from the 'Y.' The Dean of Women came too."

"Oh," Yuki said. That didn't sound terribly interesting to her, but Mother was anxious to know more.

"What did they have to say, Kenichi?" she asked. "Was it about school?"

"Oh, they said a lot of things," he said briefly. Ken seemed reluctant to say more, and soon they moved into the mess hall and the talk turned to other things. Emi and her grandparents sat with them as they usually did, and once again Mr. Kurihara was unhappy about something.

"I hear there's going to be an election," he said, contemplating his supper. "It seems the camp is being divided into five precincts and we are to elect representatives from each one to serve on a camp-wide council."

"That sounds fair and reasonable," Mother said.

But Emi's grandfather shrugged. "They say we Issei are finally going to be able to vote, but what's the use of voting in Tanforan. It's only a temporary racetrack town and we'll probably be out of here by fall."

Yuki didn't like to hear such talk. She didn't want to think about being moved again, and what was wrong with being able to vote anyway? If her mouth hadn't been full, she might have said so to Mr. Kurihara. As it was, she could only give him what she considered a disapproving look.

"Well, it's a beginning anyway," Ken said. "Maybe someday the Issei will be permitted to become citizens and be able to vote on the outside too."

Mr. Kurihara shrugged. "When this war ends, I may just go back to Japan," he murmured. "At least I won't be an enemy alien there."

It was Emi who suddenly spoke up, her face flushed, her voice rising. "Well, I'm not going with you if you do," she said defiantly. And she picked up her dishes, marched to the dish-washing area where she quickly washed her dishes in the tub of soapy water, and left the building. She hadn't even waited for dessert.

"Good for Emi!" Yuki said, but not in a very loud voice. She had never heard Emi speak out like that to her grandfather and she felt proud of her. Mr. Kurihara was too full of bitterness and Emi was right not to have any part of it. Yuki couldn't save any of the chocolate pudding for Emi, but she took the cookie that came with it for her. And then she remembered the cake and cookies that their neighbors had brought.

"Hey, Ken," she said brightly. "Let's have a party tonight."

"Great," he said quickly. "Maybe there'll be something to celebrate."

"Like what?"

72

"You'll find out," Ken said, and he quickly got in line to wash his dishes, striding on ahead so he could round up Jim and his friends.

"Stop by and invite Mr. Toda too," Mother called after him.

"OK," Ken called back.

"And Reverend and Mrs. Wada, if you see them," Mother added. But by then Ken was gone. Yuki was glad he hadn't heard. After all, there was only one cake, and it would stretch only so far.

It wasn't until Jim and some other friends came back to the stall with Ken that Yuki learned what Ken had been excited about. The deans from the university had been here to urge the students to leave camp as quickly as permitted and finish their education.

"They told us about scholarships that would be available in colleges in the midwest and back east where Japanese are permitted to be free," Jim explained. "We're all thinking about applying and getting out."

"You too?" Yuki asked Ken.

Ken looked down at his shoes. "Well, I was thinking about it," he admitted.

"You mean you'd leave Mama and me here and go out by yourself?"

Ken didn't want to answer. He was torn between wanting to go out to finish school and staying to look after Mother and Yuki until Father returned.

But Mother eased his mind. "Of course you must go out if you have the opportunity," she said quickly. "Father would want you to do that and so would I."

"But I wouldn't," Yuki blurted out. It would be terrible to

have Ken leave, and besides the last thing Father had said was for Ken to look after her and Mother.

There was a knock on the door and Mr. Toda arrived with a small bag of peanuts for Yuki. Yuki thanked him politely, but not even that, or the thought of the delicious chocolate cake with nuts and marshmallows could cheer Yuki now. There was no further talk about scholarships or finishing school, but Ken had already spoiled the evening for Yuki and she felt as though a great black cloud had suddenly descended to engulf her in its gloom.

9
A
New
Rumor

HALF asleep, Yuki heard the sounds of waking all around her and knew it was six thirty. The headcounter was making his rounds, pounding at each stall door until someone answered with the number of people inside.

"It's a stupid idea," Ken remarked when the headcount began. "No one's going to try to escape."

Yuki thought he was right. It did seem silly. After all, how far could anyone with a Japanese face get on the outside? Still, it was an order from someone, somewhere, and each morning they were roused at six thirty and had to be back in their stall for another headcount at six thirty in the evening as well. Since Ken slept closest to the door, it was his job to answer "Three" whenever the headcounter came.

This morning Yuki was wide awake, ready to call out to the headcounter if Ken were still asleep. Now that schools had opened, Yuki had to get up early. Even so, it was usually Emi who called to her first over the partition. "Are you ready, Yuki?" she would shout, and Yuki would answer, "In a minute, Emi. Give me one more minute." It was a good thing it took only five minutes to walk to school.

Most classes were doubled up in barracks that were meant to be mess halls, the high school met in the grandstand by the pari-mutuel windows, supplies were short, and Nisei teachers were still being recruited from among the evacuees. In spite of all that, Yuki was glad to be back in school, for she was getting bored drifting about aimlessly all day. She liked her young Nisei teacher and, after a while, got used to the strangeness of being in a school where all the pupils were Japanese.

She had wakened early this morning after dreaming that Ken was gone. The good dreams about home vanished like smoke in a night sky, but the bad dreams seemed to linger on, hovering over her early waking hours like a reluctant vulture. Yuki shuddered and tried to brush away the loneliness left by the dream.

Ever since the night of the party, she wanted to ask Ken whether he had applied for a scholarship, but he didn't seem to want to discuss it with her. Now Yuki was afraid that everything was already settled and that he had made up his mind to go.

"Grandfather will look after you," Emi said, trying to console Yuki.

But Yuki wasn't so sure she wanted to be looked after by Mr. Kurihara. He might even try to talk Mother into going back to Japan someday.

"We have many friends in camp," Mother reminded her. "And besides, Father may be home one of these days." He had written that there would soon be hearings for all the men, and his Caucasian friends had written many affidavits of support for him.

Mother seemed pleased about Ken's efforts to leave camp. "We must think of his future," she explained. "We want him to be a fine doctor someday."

Still, Yuki didn't want him to go. The more she thought of it, the sadder she felt.

It didn't help matters when she came home from school and saw the college catalogs that had come in the mail for Ken. Mother saw Yuki's glum face and knew what was troubling her.

"Come help me weed our little garden," she urged. Like many of their neighbors, Mother had sent out for some flower seeds and planted them in a small patch of ground in front of their stall. The summer sun and the manure-rich soil had produced a beautiful crop of stocks, petunias, and zinnias that brightened the patch of earth around them. Mother said she would rather have flowers to look at than laundered clothes and she didn't have clothes lines put up in front of their stall as many of the people had done.

Even digging in the soil with the sun warm on her back and the bright zinnias blinking at her didn't seem to help. It wasn't just feeling lonely, it was the thought that Ken was deserting them that bothered Yuki most. Ken was not only letting her down, he was breaking his promise to Father.

"Phooie! Double phooie!" Yuki murmured, and leaving Mother to finish weeding, she decided to go to the canteen.

Yuki didn't even bother asking Emi to go with her. She simply ran down the track, squinting at the dust and wind and hurried to the canteen. It was crowded as usual, and Yuki took her place in line, counting to see how many tickets there were in the two-and-a-half dollar script book which was issued to each adult for the month. Mother had had to wait in line for two hours to get her script.

When Yuki finally got to the counter, the only items left were black and brown shoelaces. "Just what I wanted," she said glumly. She had just missed out on the last of the ice cream.

Suddenly, she felt a light tap on her shoulder. "Why do you look so sad, little one? Did you have your heart set on some ice cream?" It was Mr. Toda who had been in line behind her.

Yuki shook her head. "Who cares about ice cream," she mumbled.

"Ah, then it is something else, is it?"

Yuki wasn't going to say anything, but the concerned look on Mr. Toda's face made her want to tell him everything. She soon found herself telling him all about Ken and his plan to leave for school.

Mr. Toda listened thoughtfully, nodding and rubbing his chin. "Ah yes," he said slowly. "It is too bad life must be filled with such difficult choices. Why must we choose between Japan and America? I love them both. I belong to both." He spoke as though he were still arguing with the bald-headed man and seemed almost to be talking to himself. "It is too bad Ken must choose between his responsibility to you and finishing school," he added. "It is a hard choice."

Yuki shook her head. "I don't think it's so hard," she said. "He should just decide to stay here."

The old man looked hard at Yuki and put a hand on her cheek. "Let him go, Yuki Chan," he said softly. "Your mother is right. You know that, don't you?" And then, patting her shoulder, he left for the Bachelors' Quarters while Yuki turned toward Barrack 16.

Deep in her heart Yuki knew that both Mother and Mr. Toda were right. She knew she should be glad for Ken, but somehow she just couldn't make herself tell him so. Besides, he was rarely home these days and he often ate his meals at other mess halls with his friends. In the evening he would go out to play ball or go to the Town Hall discussion group or a recorded concert with Jim and the boys, and on Saturdays, he usually got dressed up and took a girl to the dance at the grandstand. Even when there were old movies at the recreation hall, he wouldn't go with Yuki and Emi, but went with his own friends. Maybe Ken was already a lost cause, Yuki thought, whether he stayed or not.

It was one afternoon in the showers that Yuki first heard the rumor that they would soon be sent to another inland camp. She and Emi had gone together and not discovered till they were half through showering that they had both forgotten to bring their bath towels.

"Oh," Emi wailed. "How'll we get dry?"

"One of us can go back for towels," Yuki suggested. "Loser gets dressed. *Jan Ken Po!*"

Wet and dripping, they clenched fists and shook three times. Emi thrust a flat palm for paper and Yuki thrust out two fingers for scissors.

"Scissors cut paper. I win," Yuki shouted.

Shrieking with laughter and dismay, Emi pulled her dress on over her dampness and ran in her *zoris* to fetch their towels. It

79

was while Yuki waited that she heard two high school girls talking about the new rumor.

"I hear we're moving in September," one called to the other.

"Where to?"

"Utah or Idaho."

"Ugh, how awful! Are you sure?"

"Everybody was talking about it in math today."

When Emi got back, Yuki quickly told her what she had heard and then offered to wait while Emi took another shower and dried herself properly. But Emi wasn't about to waste her time on a second shower.

"Let's go find out if it's true," she said eagerly. "Grandma will know. She knows all about every rumor in camp."

When Emi and Yuki rushed back to tell her, however, Emi's grandmother scarcely looked up from the sweater she was knitting to enter in the camp Hobby Show.

"Oh, I've heard that rumor for days now," she said calmly, "but I don't believe it's going to happen for a long time."

When Ken came home for the six thirty headcount, he said everyone at the hospital was talking about the same rumor. "They say it'll happen within a month," he said soberly. And then after a brief silence, he spoke again.

"Well, I guess that settles it," he said. "I'm not going out to college. At least, not yet."

"But Kenichi," Mother objected. "We have friends here. We'll all be moving together. You needn't worry about Yuki and me."

Ken had made up his mind, however, with the same determination that Mother often displayed. "I'm not leaving you two to

pack up and leave here by yourselves," he said flatly. "Jim's decided he should stay and help his family too. Besides," he added with a grin, "who else would carry that enormous rucksack of ours but me?"

Yuki wanted to rush over and give Ken an enormous hug, but she knew he would hate such a display of affection.

"Yahoo!" she shouted happily, and she didn't care how far down the stable anyone heard. "Ken's not leaving! Ken's going to stay!"

"Hooray!" Emi shouted from her stall and she came rushing over to celebrate with Yuki.

"Thank you, Kenichi," Mother said, and although she said nothing more, she looked relieved and happy.

Yuki simply had to do something nice for Ken. She went to her shelf and got out a chocolate bar from Mimi that she'd been saving for herself. She was tempted to break it in half and go halves with Ken, but in a burst of generosity, she gave him the whole bar.

"Here," she said, thrusting it into his hand. "You can have it. It's got almonds in it."

Ken knew what Yuki was trying to tell him. "Thanks," he said simply, and grinning, he gave her a friendly poke in the ribs.

10
Goodbye, Canforan

*Y*UKI sat scrunched on the floor, leaning against her cot piled high now with all the things that had to be packed into her suitcases once more. She hated the mess that each move created.

"Isn't it awful?" she wrote to Mimi. "We're being sent to Utah, everything in camp is closing down, and Ken's taken all the furniture apart to make crates. So here I am writing to you on the floor!"

It was going to be sad to leave this funny patched-together city of horse stalls and barracks, and Yuki knew that as much as she had complained about their dark crowded stall, she was actually going to miss it. After all, it had been home for four months and it *was* in California.

Yuki's thoughts jumped from one thing to another as she tried to straighten out the jumble in her mind and put it down on paper. She looked at the diary she'd been keeping to see what had happened since she last wrote to Mimi. There had been the

83

FBI inspection one day and then the Army inspection for contraband when they'd been confined to their quarters all day. Yuki remembered how Emi's grandmother had missed the search because she'd gone to the latrine at just the wrong moment, and the soldiers who stood guard around their barrack wouldn't let her back in.

"We're being searched and inspected inside out," Yuki wrote as she reached the second page of Mimi's letter. "I wonder what in the world they think we're hiding. Diamonds, maybe, or guns?"

Not even Emi's grandfather would have a gun in his possession in spite of all the grumbling he did.

"Well, anyway," she went on, "we're being shipped out of Tanforan by mess hall groups and our turn will be coming pretty soon. Before we go," she added, "please, puh-leeze, find out how Pepper is."

It was strange that Andy had never written after his first letter telling them that Pepper was fine. And this was the third time she'd asked Mimi to check on him too. It was as though they'd all forgotten that Pepper even existed.

At last it was Mrs. Jamieson who wrote to her in big strokes that slanted boldly over the paper. "Mimi couldn't bear to write to you, so I promised that I would instead," she began. "My dear sweet Yuki, your beloved Pepper is dead. I believe he died peacefully in his sleep. Don't grieve, my love. Perhaps he has met up with my old parrot, wherever it is that pets go, and who knows, maybe my good Captain is looking after them both."

Yuki could barely finish reading the letter. She ran out of the stall and headed for the farthest corner of camp where she was not likely to see anyone she knew. She leaned against the foot of one of the watchtowers and let the tears come, sobbing into her wet grimy palms until she heard voices approaching, and then she ran on. One of the worst things about being in camp was that there was no place to go to be alone. Wherever she went, people pressed close—in her own stall, at the mess hall, at school, on the track, even in the latrines and washroom. There was nowhere one could go to be all alone.

Yuki wished she could climb up into one of the eucalyptus trees and hide inside a cluster of its crescent-shaped leaves. Pepper was gone and there was nowhere she could go to grieve for him. Yuki slumped to the ground and sat on the sun-dried weeds that grew at the edge of the camp. She turned her back to the barracks and the stables and all the people. She buried her face in her arms and didn't go back to her stall until it was long past time for supper.

When it became official that their mess hall group would be leaving for Utah in a few days, Mother got up every morning before five o'clock in order to find an empty tub to do her laundry.

"Why does everybody have to have clean clothes just to go to Utah?" Yuki asked.

But Mother was like everyone else. "I've got to wash while I can," she said urgently. "We may not even have hot water in Utah, and besides, I don't want to pack a lot of dirty sheets and towels."

Soon it was their last day in Tanforan and their last day in California. The small mess halls were now closed and supper was at four thirty for the departing contingent at the grandstand mess hall.

Yuki's stomach felt just as it did the morning they left Berkeley. It just didn't want any food, and that was a strange state for it after feeling deprived so often. Yuki pushed the sweet spareribs around on her plate, but before she could eat them, it was time to hurry back to their stall. They would pick up their baggage and then report to the laundry barrack which had been fenced off as the departure area. Beyond it, outside the barbedwire fence, a train had been pulled up to a siding ready to transport them, the second contingent of five hundred people, from Tanforan to Topaz, Utah.

Jim Hirai came to help Ken tie up the rucksack and to help with their other baggage, and Mr. Toda came clutching a bunch of flowers that the camp gardeners were giving away now that the gardens would soon be plowed under.

"Well, we'd better get moving," Ken urged.

Yuki took one last look around the stall. Now with all their belongings gone, it looked barren and empty, and she no longer felt very sad about leaving it.

The last minute things that wouldn't fit into their suitcases were squeezed into knitting and shopping bags, and looking like refugees laden with all their worldly possessions, they were finally ready to start for the departure area.

"Ready, Emi?" Yuki called.

"I am, but Grandma isn't," Emi called back.

Yuki soon saw why she had taken so long. In each hand, Emi's grandmother had an enormous bundle wrapped in large squares of cloth, and then tied to her back like an extra child was still another bundle. Mrs. Kurihara was like a squirrel expecting a harsh winter. She had saved scraps of wood, wire, string, nails, dried grass, leftover crackers and cookies and dried fruit, and had

stuffed everything into her bulging bags in spite of Mr. Kurihara's objections.

"You wait," she said to Emi and Yuki who couldn't help but
giggle at the sight of her, "everything will be useful in Utah and
then you will thank me for being so foresighted."

She had even filled her bath barrel with possessions, put a lid
on it, and shipped it to Utah. "You're always welcome to borrow
it whenever you want a bath," she reminded Yuki and Mother.

There was such a crowd at the departure area, they could
barely say goodbye to Jim and Mr. Toda and their other friends
who would be following them to Utah. There was a mad jumble
of people, baggage, and crying children, and before Yuki knew
what was happening, they were swept inside the fence toward
the baggage inspection area.

"Oh no," Ken groaned, "not another inspection!"

"Stay together now," Mother said, taking hold of Yuki's hand.
"We don't want to get separated."

But even as she spoke, Yuki heard Emi shout, "Where's
Grandma?"

Yuki turned to look, and sure enough, Mrs. Kurihara with all
her bundles had suddenly disappeared.

Emi wanted to go look for her, but Mr. Kurihara shook his
head. "Stay with me," he said firmly. "Your grandmother is a
wanderer, but she'll be back. She will find us."

They were divided into numbered groups and told to sit on
rows of benches until it was time to board the train. They waited
one hour and still Mrs. Kurihara had not returned. Now even
Emi's grandfather seemed a little worried, for they couldn't possi-
bly leave without her.

Soon a murmur swept through the crowd as a group captain announced that they were to file through a double row of armed Military Police to board the train.

"Grandma!" Yuki heard Emi call out. And there she was at last carrying still another bundle, her face flushed and wet with perspiration.

"Such a big bother!" she said puffing. "All I did was go back for something I'd forgotten under my cot, and then they wouldn't let me back inside the departure area so I roamed about a bit and found all these nice dried weeds I can use for weaving some sun hats." She looked so pleased with herself that even Mr. Kurihara couldn't be angry with her.

"We've been so worried about you," Mother said, but Mrs. Kurihara seemed surprised that they had even missed her.

"Why, I wouldn't have missed the train," she explained calmly. "I knew it would be at least an hour before they'd let us on anyway, so I made good use of the time."

And, as usual, Grandmother Kurihara was right. She stepped briskly toward the MPs and boarded the train as though it had been held until now especially for her.

The train was an old one, with gaslight fixtures and seats hard enough to have been pews in an old Puritan church.

"Wow, wonder where they dug up this relic?" Ken said as he hurried to find a good window seat for them.

Yuki pressed her nose up against the window and saw the vast crowd of remaining evacuees who had come to see them off for Utah. As she watched, trying to spot some familiar faces, the train whistle blew and all the hands began to wave like a sea of wind-blown grass.

"Goodbye everybody . . . Goodbye Tanforan . . . Goodbye California," Yuki called softly.

The train gave a lurch and lumbered slowly northward, leaving behind the stables and the barracks and the windswept cluster of eucalyptus trees. Yuki waved until she could no longer see the watchtowers, and then she turned her attention to all the things she hadn't seen for four months.

"Look," she cried excitedly. There were houses and gardens and stores and cars and dogs and cats and children with blond and brown hair playing and riding bicycles.

What thrilled her most, however, was the sight of San Francisco Bay and the bridge that spanned it. It was growing dark now and Yuki could see the string of lights that seemed to float over the water. The bridge was peaceful and magnificent, untouched by the war and its clamor, sparkling across the bay like a golden jewel. As Yuki looked, she was filled with longing for all that was past. She thought of home and the good times they'd had and of being happy as they drove over the bridge to go to San Francisco. It seemed everyone else was thinking similar thoughts, for the car grew very still as people strained to keep the bridge in sight as long as possible. No one spoke, for there didn't seem to be any words to say what everyone was feeling.

Suddenly, the car captain's voice broke the silent web of memories in which they had all been tangled up for a few moments.

"Shades down everybody," he said. "All shades must be drawn from sundown to sunrise. The lights are going on now. Shades down please."

He walked up and down the aisle, waiting until each person

had reluctantly pulled the shade to shut out the world beyond the window. When he had gone by, however, Yuki lifted the edge of her shade and poked her head through the small space she had made, watching the neon signs flash by. As she peered out, she began to feel a growing excitement.

"Hey, Ken," she said eagerly, "we're outside the barbed wire! We're in the outside world!"

"Yeah, great," he said. But there was no enthusiasm in his voice.

"Utah might be nice," Yuki went on, undaunted.

"Not likely," he growled.

"What's wrong?" Yuki asked. Ken had seemed cheerful enough until a few moments ago.

But Mother seemed to know what troubled him. "Ken just needs to be back in the world," she said quietly.

Yuki looked hard at Ken who was now stretched out on the opposite seat, his knees bent so he could squeeze the length of his body on the short seat, his arms locked beneath his head for a pillow. His eyes were closed, but Yuki knew he wasn't asleep.

Maybe he was thinking about what Emi's grandfather had said that morning, Yuki thought. Mr. Kurihara had said America was making prisoners of its own citizens, inspecting them, searching them, and herding them like cattle from one camp to another.

But she remembered too what Mother had said back to him. "Fear has made this country do something she will one day regret, Mr. Kurihara, but we cannot let this terrible mistake poison our hearts. If we do, then we will be the ones to destroy ourselves and our children as well. Don't you see?" Mother had said. "We must make the best of it."

Mama was right, Yuki thought. Mr. Kurihara was wrong. Still, his words must have sunk into Ken's head and stayed there like a bothersome fly.

"Ken," Yuki called once more. She wanted to tell him to apply for a scholarship and go out to school as soon as they got to Utah. But Ken wouldn't answer. He had closed his mind to everything around him, including Yuki. And so the moment passed and Yuki never said the words that might have given him some comfort.

11

A Home
in the
Desert

THEY rode all night and through the next day and still another night before they reached Utah. Yuki had never spent two more miserable nights in all her life. The train was hot and stuffy, the water ran out, and the seats grew harder every minute. Yuki squirmed and wriggled and yawned and stretched and finally poked Mother to see if she was still up too.

The only span of relief had come in the second morning when the train pulled to a stop in the middle of a barren Nevada desert and everyone was permitted to get off to stretch and breathe some fresh air for a few minutes. Even in the midst of the desert, however, they were guarded by a row of armed soldiers as though they were prisoners who might try to escape.

When at last they arrived at Delta, Utah, Yuki was so stiff she could scarcely walk to the buses that were lined up waiting to take them on the last leg of the journey to Topaz.

Everyone was hot and tired and sleepless, and even Emi's grandmother seemed to have lost her energy. Yuki noticed how pale Emi looked and how quiet she had grown during the journey. She hadn't even wanted to play cards with her and Yuki had finally wheedled Ken into a game of Hearts.

When they were seated in the buses and saw the surrounding countryside, however, there was a general lifting of spirits.

"Topaz is such a beautiful golden name," Mother said hopefully, "it surely can't be too bad a place. And look," she added cheerfully, "everything looks so fresh and green."

There were houses with flowering gardens and leafy shade trees and fields full of growing things. Yuki began to feel better. If Topaz was going to be like this, it might be a wonderful place.

"Didn't I tell you Utah might be nice?" she asked Ken. But he was saving his opinion for later.

"We're not in Topaz yet," he observed.

The buses moved quickly through the small town, passed a few farms, and then entered the Sevier Desert. Gradually the trees and the grass and the flowers began to disappear. Soon there was no vegetation at all and they were surrounded by a vast gray-white desert where nothing grew except dry clumps of greasewood.

The eager hopeful voices on the bus died down and soon stopped altogether. Mother said nothing more and Yuki herself grew silent. At the western rim of the desert they could see a tall range of mountains, but long before they reached their sheltering shadows the buses made a sharp left turn, and there in the midst of the desert, they came upon rows and rows of squat tar-papered barracks sitting in a pool of white dust that had once been the

94

bottom of a lake. They had arrived at Topaz, the Central Utah War Relocation Center, which would be their new home.

Ken turned to look at Yuki. "Well, here we are," he said dryly. "This is beautiful Topaz."

The minute Yuki stepped off the bus, she felt the white powdery dust of the desert engulf her like a smothering blanket. The Boy Scout Drum and Bugle Corp had come out to welcome the incoming buses, but now they looked like flour-dusted cookies that had escaped from a bakery.

Yuki coughed while one of the team of doctors inspected her throat and then she ran quickly to talk to Emi while Ken finished registering the family.

"We've been assigned to Block 7, Barrack 2, Apartment C," she informed her. "Try to get the room next door."

Emi nodded. "OK, I'll tell Grandma," she said, for they both knew that if anybody could manage such an arrangement, Grandma could.

A boy about Ken's age offered to take them out to their new quarters. He had come in one of the earlier contingents and already knew his way around the big, sprawling barrack city.

"It's a mile square," he explained as they started toward Block 7, and like a guide on a tour he told them all he knew about Topaz.

"There're forty-two blocks and each block has twelve barracks with a mess hall and a latrine-washroom in the center," he pointed out. "When the barracks are all finished and occupied, we'll be the fifth largest city in Utah."

"Imagine!" Mother said.

It sounded impressive, but Yuki thought she had never seen a

96

more dreary place in all her life. There wasn't a single tree or a blade of grass to break the monotony of the sun-bleached desert. It was like the carcass of a chicken stripped clean of any meat and left all dry, brittle bone. The newly constructed road was still soft with churned up dust and they sank into it with each step as though they were plowing through a snow bank.

"Whoever built this camp wasn't very bright," Ken observed as they struggled along.

"Why?" Yuki asked, although she could think of several reasons herself. For one thing, she certainly wouldn't have covered all the barracks with black tarpaper. It made the camp look so bleak and uninviting. She would have painted the barracks all different colors. Maybe one block would be pink and lavender with rose-colored chimneys and roofs, and another block would be blue and green with some sunny yellow roofs. "Why?" she asked Ken again.

"If they'd left some of the greasewood growing, the roots would have held down some of the dust," he explained. "As it is, they've churned up this whole camp site like one big sack of loose flour."

"You're right," their guide agreed. "You should see one of our dust storms. You'll wish you'd never heard of Topaz when you've been in one of those."

Yuki shuddered. It sounded horrible. It was bad enough even without the wind, for the dust just hung in the air, sifting into her eyes and into her nose and mouth with each breath.

Mother was holding a handkerchief over her nose and mouth so Yuki could see only her eyes, her lashes fringed with dust. The sun blazed down on them making Yuki feel dry and parched

97

deep down inside. Her heart felt shriveled and her lungs seemed to be drying up. Her head felt light, as though it were floating on somebody else's body, and when the guide said something about the altitude, his voice sounded far away.

"Well, here we are," he said at last. "Your room is in the center of the barrack. The center rooms are for smaller families, the end rooms for couples and the ones in between are for big families."

Yuki was glad to see that their new room was bigger than the horse stall, measuring about eighteen by twenty, but it was just as bleak. There was nothing in the room except three army cots. The inner sheetrock walls hadn't yet been installed, so dust had filtered into the room from every crack in the siding and around the windows. It covered the floor, gathered in drifts in the corners, and hung in the air so that Yuki could taste it in her mouth.

Their guide pointed to the small black pot-bellied stoves that stood outside their door, warning, "Don't touch those stoves until the crews come to install them, and don't put up any shelves yet because you'll just have to take them down when they put in the sheetrock walls and ceiling. OK?"

Ken nodded. "OK. Thanks."

"Well, good luck," the young boy said, and he left quickly as though he didn't want to be around when they began to feel discouraged.

Mother sat down carefully on the dust-covered springs of one of the cots and looked around. "I suppose we should look for a broom," she said wearily, but she didn't seem to have the heart to start cleaning.

Yuki flopped down on another of the cots and glanced through the instruction sheet that was given to them when they registered.

"Listen," she said, reading aloud, " 'You are now in Topaz, Utah. Here we say dining hall, not mess hall; Safety Council, not Internal Police; residents, not evacuees, and last but not least, mental climate, not morale.' "

Ken groaned. "Never mind," he objected. "I don't want to hear any more of that junk."

But Yuki went on reading to Mother that there would eventually be four bathtubs installed in each block. "Emi's grandmother will be glad," she said with a grin, "and listen, it says there'll be individual basins too. No more tin troughs!"

Yuki felt cheered enough to do some investigating. "I'll go see if it's as good as they say," she said, hurrying off to make an inspection. She discovered, however, that the facilities were still far from complete. There were no seats on the toilets, no hot water in the laundry, and no lights anywhere. And while Yuki was splashing cold water on her face, the water became a weak dribble and then stopped completely. Their water supply was coming from nearby artesian wells and already it was strained from overuse.

Yuki went back to their barrack and reported her findings. "You know something, Mama," she said bleakly, "my 'mental climate' is lousy."

"Well, Topaz isn't exactly a summer resort, Yuki," Ken answered, and he went off to look for some mattresses and a broom.

It took several days for them to get used to the heat and altitude of Topaz. The doctors gave out salt tablets, but they only made Yuki feel worse, and she stopped eating altogether when the refrigerators broke and the entire block came down with food poisoning.

It was so cold in the mornings that Yuki wore her heaviest slacks and sweater, but by afternoon even her summer shorts felt hot. It was as though summer and winter had gotten mixed up and arrived together here in the desert to confuse and confound them. The time Yuki liked best was just after sunset when the air was still and the sky became a roaring blaze of color. The desert sky, uncluttered by city smoke, was the most beautiful sight Yuki had ever seen. She loved the night sky too when the stars danced across the vast blackness and seemed almost to rush toward her in their dazzling brilliance. The stars seemed much closer than in Berkeley and the moon was an enormous yellow-orange ball that looked like a nighttime sun. Yuki felt sure there must be some poetry in the desert sky, but the right words didn't seem to come even to Mother.

Emi and her grandparents lived in the same block two barracks away. Often after supper, Yuki and Mother would meet Emi and her grandmother outside the mess hall and together they would walk along the northern edge of the camp just beyond their block. As they walked, they could see the camp hospital with its black smokestack and the watchtowers that rose high above the cluster of barracks. Just beyond the barbed-wire fence, they could see the barracks of the Military Police and sometimes, they would hear them singing in the still desert air. "I suppose they are lonely too," Mother would say softly. "Surely they cannot be happy here either, so far from home."

On this particular warm evening, they walked with their eyes on the distant mountains, watching them gradually disappear into the growing darkness. Emi and Yuki walked along ahead of Mother and Mrs. Kurihara, hearing only the soft murmur of their voices behind them. Emi scuffled her toes in the dust, keeping her head down and watching the ground.

"Why do you keep looking at your feet?" Yuki asked. "The sky's a lot prettier."

"I know," Emi answered, "but Grandpa found two arrowheads in the ground near our barrack and he says this whole area must be full of interesting things. The man next door found a fossilized trilobite and I'm looking for one for Grandpa."

Now Yuki found herself watching the ground as well. It would be fun to find an old arrowhead chiseled from stone hundreds of years ago by some Indian warrior. It made her blood tingle to think of Indians hunting and fishing around what once was a great salt lake and she wondered what they would think now to find their lake all dried up with thousands of Japanese living upon it. Yuki was so caught up in searching the ground now that she didn't notice how much Emi was coughing or how pale she looked in spite of all the sun.

As suddenly as the wind that sprang from the desert to sweep through Topaz, Emi fell to the ground like a small sack, crumpling soundlessly in a tiny heap.

"Emi!" Yuki shouted.

Her grandmother and Mother rushed to her side. "Emi Chan, what has happened? Emi Chan!"

Yuki looked up and saw the camp hospital a hundred yards away. "I'll go find a doctor," she said and ran on rubbery legs, panting and gasping and stumbling in the soft dust.

Before she had gotten half way, she saw two men in white coats coming toward her. They were doctors from the hospital coming off duty and returning to their barracks.

"Help!" Yuki shouted, scarcely knowing how to begin telling them what happened. She pointed to Emi and the two women hovering over her, and the doctors, seeing Yuki's frightened face, knew what to do. They ran to Emi and bent over her. By the time Yuki caught up with them, they were feeling her pulse and lifting her eyelids and telling Mrs. Kurihara that they'd carry her to the hospital.

"Don't worry," one of the doctors reassured them. "It's probably just heat prostration."

But Yuki felt a sudden chill come over her, and the mild evening desert breeze seemed now to hold the cold breath of night.

12

Dust
Storm

"WAIT here," the doctor said quietly. "We'll try to find a bed for the little girl."

Yuki almost felt sick herself as she watched them take Emi away. It was terrible to see her so limp and lifeless, when only a few minutes ago she had been talking with her about arrowheads and trilobites.

"Do you think Emi will be all right?" she whispered anxiously to her mother.

Mother nodded. "I'm sure she will," she said. "We'll know soon."

Yuki turned to Emi's grandmother, but for once Mrs. Kurihara didn't seem to have anything to say. She sat silent and hunched on a stiff folding chair, rubbing her hands together as though she were terribly cold. She didn't even seem to notice all the people and baggage and cots that crowded the hospital corridor. The camp had run out of completed barracks for the people who continued to arrive from Tanforan, and after using all the

103

available laundry barracks, they were now bringing people to sleep in the hospital corridors. The new arrivals looked bewildered and forlorn, and Yuki felt sorry for them. It seemed a silly business to keep bringing people into a camp that wasn't even ready for them, and Yuki was glad they had their own room even if it was barren and dusty.

Everyone around her looked tired, and feeling weary herself, Yuki leaned on Mother's shoulder and closed her eyes. With the buzz of voices and the antiseptic hospital smells drifting around her, she fell asleep, awaking with a start when she heard the doctor's voice.

"We'll keep her here overnight and run some tests," he explained briefly. "You can look in on her now if you like." And then he was gone.

They tiptoed to the ward where Emi was asleep, her face flushed and her hair damp. She was coughing a dry raspy cough even in her sleep.

"Oh dear," Mrs. Kurihara said miserably. "She doesn't look at all well."

And she didn't. Yuki had a dreadful feeling that Emi was a lot sicker than any of them cared to admit.

Yuki was told that Emi wasn't to have any visitors, but the next afternoon she went to see her anyway. After all, she was her best friend, and what good was a friend who stayed away when you were sick. Besides, she had found a trilobite in the sand near their mess hall and she knew it would make Emi happy.

Yuki tried not to look nervous as she went into the hospital. She marched in the front door as though she belonged there and headed straight for Emi's ward. The corridors were still crowded with people and no one seemed to know who belonged there and who didn't. Yuki hurried to Emi's bed and found her staring at the ceiling, her eyes bright with fever and her face still flushed.

"Hi," Yuki whispered softly. "You all right?"

Emi was surprised to see her. "Golly, I sure am glad you came," she said weakly. "I thought nobody could come except Grandma and Grandpa."

Yuki put a finger to her lips. "I'm not supposed to be here, but nobody even noticed me." She dug into the pocket of her skirt and put the small gray trilobite in Emi's damp hand. "It's for you to keep," she said grandly. "It's my get-well present to you."

Emi smiled happily. "Thanks. I'm not going to let Grandpa have this one," she said. "This one's going to be mine." And then she began to cough once more.

Yuki ducked as a nurse came into the ward with a trayful of medicine. "I'll be back," she whispered, and then making herself as small as possible, she darted quickly from the room.

As she opened the hospital doors, a hot wind roared across the desert, pulling the door from her grasp and flinging dust everywhere. The sky was a strange murky gray, blending completely with the sand below so the whole world seemed to be a gray-white mass. Yuki gasped and drew back. She was facing her first Topaz dust storm and she remembered uneasily what their guide had said the day they'd arrived.

Should she wait at the hospital until it was over? But suppose it lasted all day. There was no way to let Mother know where she was. Yuki decided to try running home. If she hurried, maybe she could get there before the storm got too bad. She

105

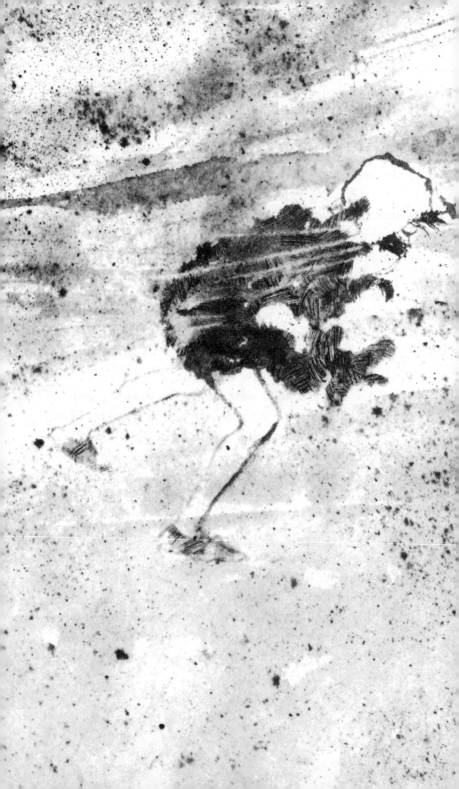

tightened the knot of her bandana, pulled one corner of it over her mouth, and then taking a deep breath, she began to run.

The wind now lifted great masses of sand from the ground and flung it into the air with such fury that Yuki could no longer see the barracks of the nearest block. Pebbles stung at her legs, and her breath came in short gulping gasps. Yuki felt smothered, and her heart began to pound as she felt terror rising inside of her. She wondered if she should turn back, but when she looked, the hospital, too, had vanished behind a thick cloud of dust.

Yuki ran now with desperation until she finally came to a barrack and could lean against it to catch her breath. Even there, however, she couldn't escape the wind and she stumbled along until she came to the laundry barrack in the center of the block. She could barely open the door, but fear now gave her strength she didn't know she had. The door slammed shut behind her and Yuki found herself in an empty laundry barrack hazy with dust. She sank down on one of the benches against the wall and caught her breath. Outside she could hear the wind still screaming and the sound of objects being thrown against the barrack walls like pieces of driftwood.

It seemed like the end of the world—at least the end of Yuki's world. As the barrack shuddered and rattled against the wind she pictured herself being flung into the desert and blown far away, never ever to see Mother or Ken or Emi or Father again.

"Help!" she shouted, but there was no one to hear her. Just when Yuki thought she couldn't bear it another minute, the wind suddenly seemed to ease up. Yuki didn't wait a single second. She dashed from the barrack and headed toward home as fast as she could run. The sand still stung at her face and she felt a terrible ache in her chest, but finally there was Block 7 just ahead and she hurried on to their barrack. She burst into their room panting and gasping and crying all at once. Mother was sitting alone on her cot, a handkerchief tied around her nose and mouth, her hair powdered with dust.

"My, I'm glad to see you," she said, giving Yuki a hug.

Yuki clung to the comfort of her mother's embrace. "I didn't think I'd ever see you again," she said, still breathless.

"Where in the world were you in all this dust and wind?" Mother asked.

If she hadn't been so unnerved by the dust storm, Yuki might not have confessed she'd sneaked into the hospital to see Emi, but now she blurted the whole story to Mother in a rush of words.

"The dust storm was horrible," she said shuddering at the thought of it, "and Emi didn't look good either."

It was then that Mother looked at Yuki and said, "I've got something to tell you, Yuki. You mustn't visit Emi Chan any more until they know for sure what's wrong with her."

"But why?" Yuki asked, puzzled.

"They think she may have tuberculosis."

"Tuberculosis," Yuki said astounded. "But nobody gets that any more with milk and butter and things like that." Or did they? Yuki felt her body go cold. Suppose Emi did have TB. "What will happen if she does have it, Mama?" Yuki asked slowly.

"I don't know," Mother said honestly. "They might have to send her out to a sanatorium." Then seeing the sadness that crossed Yuki's face, she added, "But then, it may not be that at all, you know. Maybe she just needs some rest and some good nourishing food."

Maybe it was her grandmother's strange juices that had made Emi sick, Yuki thought. Mrs. Kurihara believed that she could cure any ailment with special herbs and powders and concoctions that she cooked up on her hot plate. Once in Tanforan when Emi couldn't shake off a bad cold in her sunless stall, her grandmother had brewed a broth and made Emi drink it every day. It was only after Emi finally recovered that she admitted it had been made by brewing earthworms.

"Oh, Grandma!" Emi had shrieked. "How could you make me drink such a horrible thing?"

But her grandmother simply shrugged and said, "It made you well when none of the doctors' pills could cure you, didn't it?"

And Emi had to admit that something had indeed made her well. Maybe it *was* Grandma's magic potion, she told Yuki.

But ever since then, Yuki was careful never to visit Mrs. Kurihara when she wasn't feeling well. And any time she offered her some tea, she smelled it to make sure it was really tea and not some terrible juice that she had brewed.

"Poor Emi," Yuki said now. If she didn't get well soon, she would miss the opening of school.

13
A
Last
Visit

"ICE!" Yuki shouted in amazement as she looked inside the kettle of water that Mother always kept on hand. "No wonder it's so cold. The water's turned to ice!"

But no one was listening. Mother had gone to wash her face and Ken was still snoring under his blanket. Yuki couldn't resist the terrible urge that suddenly came over her. She carefully lifted the thin circle of ice from the kettle and laid it on top of Ken's forehead.

"There," she said, giggling. "Wake up, Kenichi Sakane! It's time to get up!"

Ken was out of bed in one great leap, shouting and running after Yuki.

"All right, Yuki," he said menacingly. "You're going to get it."

"Help!" Yuki screamed, and darting quickly around the furniture, she ran laughing from the room. It was a good thing she was dressed and Ken wasn't. She was still breathless when she got to the washroom and saw Mother talking to Emi's grandmother. Their heads were close and their faces serious. They were speaking in whispers and Yuki knew it must be about Emi. For days now, the doctors had been taking tests and X-rays, but no one had told Yuki what was wrong.

"Can Emi come home soon?" she asked Mrs. Kurihara. "Is she all right?"

Emi's grandmother shook her head. "Emi is still sick," she said lamely. "I'm afraid you won't be able to visit her for a while."

"Will she . . . I mean, will they send her to a sanatorium?"

Mrs. Kurihara shook her head. "Thank goodness, no. The doctors say they can cure her here. There is good medicine now for tuberculosis, you know."

Yuki gasped. Then it was TB. Her grandmother had said it and now Yuki knew.

Mother put a comforting arm around the old woman's shoulder. "Of course they have good medicine," she said. "And with rest and proper food, Emi will recover quickly for she is young and eager to be well."

All day long Yuki thought about Emi lying in the hospital. How sad for her, she thought. Still, maybe it was a good thing she was someplace warm for the school barracks were far from complete and everyone huddled in coats and boots and scarves trying to keep warm. The inner sheetrock walls hadn't yet been installed and some of the barracks still had holes in the roofs where the stove chimneys were to go.

112

"If we're going to be covered with dust anyway," Yuki's teacher said one cold morning, "we may as well be a little warmer," and she took them outside to have their lessons sitting in the sun.

"It's a crazy school," Yuki wrote to Emi. "I'm beginning to think you're lucky to be in a nice warm bed instead of freezing in that dusty, drafty old barrack."

Yuki usually took her letters to Emi's grandparents instead of asking Ken to take them, even though he was now working at the hospital as an orderly. Actually, she didn't have much choice, for Ken never seemed to be around these days. He came home to sleep and he was there for the weekly headcount on Mondays, but otherwise, he spent all his time at the hospital or with Jim and his other friends. He didn't even eat at their mess hall anymore.

Yuki missed the old cheerful, gentle Ken of Berkeley. Somehow he seemed to be growing more distant and inward and never had much to say to either Mother or Yuki any more. Whenever Mother asked if he wasn't going to do something about going out to college, he just shrugged and said, "My mind's gone into deep freeze. I don't think I could study any more even if I tried."

Mr. Toda tried to talk to Ken too. "If your mind is frozen, then unfreeze it," he said sternly. "You have an obligation to your family and to yourself to finish your education. This isn't the end of the world, you know, and someday the war will end."

But Ken wouldn't even listen to the old man. "I'm learning a lot as an orderly," he said acidly, "and think of the money I'm making!"

"Kenichi, that's enough of your sarcasm," Mother snapped at

113

him. Ken had never been rude to Mr. Toda before, and Yuki saw the pained look that crossed the old man's face.

Yuki wished she had never stopped Ken from going out to college when he wanted to. Maybe now he would never become a doctor and it would all be her fault.

These days when Yuki felt the need to be comforted, she often went to visit Emi's grandparents. They missed Emi terribly, and they treated Yuki as though she was their own grandchild. Mr. Kurihara had even begun taking her with him on his long walks when he went in search of arrowheads and trilobites, showing her how to find them in the sand. He didn't talk very much, but Yuki was beginning to understand him better. She discovered that he really didn't mean half of the grumbling noises he made and that deep inside he was quite kind and gentle. In fact, he was much like Mr. Toda that way. Beneath their gruff exterior they both had kindly souls. It was just that it took a while to get inside of them to find out.

"Anyway," Yuki mused to Mother, "I like him now."

"Who?"

"Emi's grandfather. He's turning out to be pretty nice."

"Why, of course he is." Mother seemed surprised that Yuki had only now discovered something she knew all along. "Of course he is," she said again.

Yuki wished she could say as much for her own brother. "Ken's getting to be a big pain," she said dismally.

"You mustn't judge him too harshly," Mother said, coming to his defense. "There is so little here to comfort the eye or the heart, and people grow quarrelsome and sullen when they are unhappy."

114

Yuki knew it wasn't just Ken. The whole camp seemed to be festering with irritability. People seemed to be overwhelmed by a despair that was fed by the harsh weather, the drab desert, and the frustration of living behind barbed wire with whole families crowded into one small room.

The schools too, were only limping along, still without proper heat or supplies. The only good thing that had happened in weeks was that the sheetrock crews had finally come to Block 7 and put inner walls and a ceiling in each of the barracks.

"Now Ken and I can fight without anybody hearing us," Yuki wrote to Emi. "And guess what else? They finally hitched up our stove! Now that the rooms are warm, maybe you could come home. Could you?"

Yuki got so excited over the prospect, she ended her letter then and there and ran with it to Emi's grandparents. She found Mrs. Kurihara brewing some herbs on her hotplate and filling the room with a sweet spicy scent that made Yuki feel giddy.

"You aren't cooking up more juices for Emi, are you?" she asked warily.

Mrs. Kurihara laughed and wiped her hands on her apron. "No, no, this is for our neighbor. I'm going to cure her cold with it."

Then holding up a tiny vial of dark black fluid, she said, "This is the one for Emi. This will make her strong and well."

"What is it?" Yuki asked, stepping back so Mrs. Kurihara wouldn't press a sample of it on her.

"Essence of egg yolk. It's pure protein," Mrs. Kurihara said proudly. "I know this will cure Emi if the doctors can't."

From the corner of the room Mr. Kurihara clucked his

tongue. "You'd better not let the doctors hear you talking that way," he warned.

Yuki felt the same way. "Could Emi come home now that our rooms are warm?" she asked, changing the subject.

Emi's grandmother brightened. "That's a fine idea," she said eagerly. "I'll ask the doctor today, and if Emi is at home, I can give her all the essence of egg yolk I please. I'll have her well in no time at all."

Mr. Kurihara didn't try to argue with her. He was busy polishing his arrowheads and perhaps hadn't even heard.

Yuki wished later that she had gone over to admire his collection and to say something nice to him, for as things turned out, that was the last time she ever had a chance to talk to him.

14

Tragedy

at

Dusk

It happened the next evening at dusk, at the time of day when people went for walks or lingered outside the mess hall after supper to talk. The air was peaceful and still, waiting for the quiet of night after a harsh day of heat and wind.

Yuki and her mother stood with Emi's grandmother, admiring the new tree that had just been planted outside the mess hall. For several weeks now, truckloads of volunteers had gotten permission to go out with picks and shovels to a river bank far beyond the barbed wire fence to bring back gravel for surfacing the roads, and saplings to plant throughout camp. All the broad firebreaks were to be lined with saplings and each block was to have a larger tree in front of its mess hall.

"Won't it be lovely to have some green in the spring?" Mother asked, looking up at the tree and picturing the pool of shade it would provide one day.

117

Mrs. Kurihara looked doubtful. "If it can survive the dust and the wind and the alkaline soil," she said. For once she was inclined to agree with her husband who gave the tree only a month to live.

"Better to look down at the ground than at that pathetic tree," he said, and he had gone off to get Mr. Toda for their usual after-supper arrowhead hunt. The two old men had become fast friends and even if they found no arrowheads at all, still they enjoyed the daily walks in companionable silence. They were walking farther and farther from the center of camp now, searching along the southern borders of the campsite.

Mrs. Kurihara invited Yuki and Mother to come see the red wool material she had found at the camp's newly opened cooperative store.

"I'm going to sew Emi a dress to welcome her home," she explained, holding the cloth up in front of her own face.

"It's beautiful," Mother said, fingering the soft wool. "Emi Chan will look lovely in it."

Yuki looked hopefully at Mrs. Kurihara. "Does that mean Emi's coming home soon?" she asked.

"I'm hoping she will," Mrs. Kurihara answered. "If I act as though she's coming home, then I believe she really will."

Emi's grandmother believed that she could make things happen by willing them to, and she was determined to get Emi home from the hospital by sheer will. She folded the cloth carefully and gave it a little pat as though Emi were already inside it.

It was at that moment that Mr. Toda came bursting into the room without even knocking. His eyes were wild and he could scarcely speak from having run so hard.

"Something terrible has happened," he gasped. "Your hus-

118

band, Mr. Kurihara . . . he . . . he . . . he has been shot!"

Yuki thought Mr. Toda had gone clean out of his mind. She had never seen him look so distraught. His face was flushed, his hair was dissheveled, and he acted as though he had gone mad.

"It happened by the fence!" he went on, holding his hand against his heaving chest. "The guard in the watchtower . . . he shot him!"

Emi's grandmother stood there unbelieving, as though she were hearing out the impossible dream of a frightened child.

"Sit down, old man. You are trembling," she said gently. "Now what is it? What happened? What are you saying?"

If the block manager hadn't come in just then to ask about a faulty stove pipe, they might all have simply sat there, believing that poor Mr. Toda had lost his mind completely.

The block manager, however, listened carefully to Mr. Toda's story. The two old men had been walking along the southern fringe of camp, close to the barbed-wire fence that ringed the barracks. Their heads were down as they searched the ground. Suddenly there had been a shot and Mr. Kurihara had crumpled to the ground just as he was reaching for an interesting stone. The guard said he had shouted from the watchtower to halt.

"But we heard nothing . . . nothing at all," Mr. Toda said bleakly.

The commotion that followed was so enormous that Yuki scarcely remembered what happened. The room suddenly filled with people and Emi's grandmother was hurried into a truck and driven to the hospital. She was gone for several hours, and when at last she returned, she stopped by at the Sakane barrack before she went to her own.

"He is dead," she said simply, and she slumped down into a

119

chair by the stove, unable to say anything more. She looked as though she were living in a nightmare.

Mother put an arm around her shoulder to comfort her, trying to think of the right words to say. "He was a victim of the war, Mrs. Kurihara," she said at last, "just as surely as the brave boys who are dying in the Pacific. He is at peace now and won't ever suffer again."

Mrs. Kurihara nodded, but Yuki wasn't sure she had heard.

"Does Emi know?" she asked softly. She wondered if Emi, lying in another bed in the hospital, knew that her grandfather had died nearby.

It was only when Yuki spoke Emi's name that Mrs. Kurihara sat up and spoke clearly. "Emi Chan knows," she said quietly. "And it was your Kenichi who helped me tell her. He was very helpful and kind at the hospital," she said.

And as though the thought of Ken's help had given her some strength, she gathered herself up and said she would go back now to her own room.

Mother and Yuki walked home with her and offered to make a pot of tea and stay with her. But the old woman shook her head.

"I am all right now," she said slowly. "Everything will be all right. My husband is at rest. He needn't fight anyone or anything any more. You are right, Mrs. Sakane. He is at peace." A quiet calm came over her face and Yuki had a feeling that the old woman was going to be all right.

"I'm glad Kenichi was helpful," Mother said softly.

Yuki nodded in the darkness. She took her mother's hand then, and together they walked back to their barrack in silence.

All of Topaz was shocked over Mr. Kurihara's death. They grieved for him because he was the first to die in this lonely desert camp and he would be the first to be buried in the desert, outside the barbed wire that had enclosed him while he was alive. They were angry because he really needn't have died and because it could have happened to any of them.

The women of the church made artificial flowers out of bright-colored crepe paper and Yuki and Mother went to help cut and paste and roll the crepe paper into clusters of brilliant flowers. They made several wreaths and a large spray to cover the plain wooden casket.

Yuki had never been so close to death before. It filled her with a chilling fear, for it held the awfulness of forever. She sat between Mother and Mr. Toda at the funeral in the camp Buddhist church, and as the priest's Japanese words floated out over her head, she thought about Pepper and about Mrs. Jamieson's Captain. If they had found each other, as Mrs. Jamieson supposed, then maybe Emi's grandfather could somehow link up with them too, even though he never knew them in life.

She felt a little better at the thought, and later, when she saw the small wooden marker in the desert with the clusters of bright paper flowers all around, she almost felt as though Emi's grandfather were standing right there with all of them. He wouldn't have cared much for all the crying, Yuki thought. And he probably would not have minded too much being left alone in the desert with the wind shifting the sand and sending the flowers fluttering away to get caught in the sage brush. He had grown quite fond of the desert. He said its vastness fascinated him even as the ocean did. Yuki knew that from the times she had walked with

121

him. Yuki looked at Mrs. Kurihara now, her head bowed low with grief, and wished she could tell all this to her, but she didn't know how. Instead, when no one was looking, Yuki took her best arrowhead from her pocket, polished it on her skirt, and pushed it quickly into the sand beside Mr. Kurihara's newly made grave.

15
Good News

THANKSGIVING came and went quietly, and although there was turkey at the mess hall, somehow all the sadness that had come to Emi's family kept Yuki from feeling very festive.

Ken, too, seemed discouraged and bitter. "What's there to be thankful for this year?" he asked.

"For being alive and well and together," Mother answered, but Ken didn't seem to care.

Then the telegram came from Father, suddenly bringing them the cheering news they had longed to hear. "BEING RELEASED ON PAROLE," it said. "WILL JOIN YOU SOON. LOVE, DAD."

"Ya-hoo!" Yuki shouted at the top of her voice. "Maybe Papa will be home for Christmas." And she didn't care if everyone in the whole barrack heard her through the sheetrock walls. She hugged Mother and danced around the room and rumpled up Ken's hair before he could object.

For the next few days, whenever there was a knock at the

123

door, Yuki ran to open it, wondering if Father would be standing there. But each time it was only a neighbor or a friend coming to ask if they'd had any further word from Father or it was the mailman with a package from outside.

Yuki wasn't too disappointed when it was a package that arrived instead of Father. Those from Mimi and Mrs. Jamieson were the most fun. Mimi's package was filled with presents for each of them as well as with evergreen branches that smelled of Christmas and green forests, and colored paper and ribbon to make decorations for the branches. "So you can make your own Christmas tree," Mimi wrote.

Mrs. Jamieson's package contained sugared nuts, homemade cookies, and a fruitcake filled with spices and nuts and raisins. Yuki could almost feel the warmth of Mrs. Jamieson's cozy house as she sniffed the spicy delicious scents of her package, and she longed for a glimpse of her old neighbor rummaging about in her bulging closets looking for something interesting to show Yuki.

Christmas in camp was a far cry from Christmas at home, but still, it wasn't too terrible. The mess halls were decorated by the kitchen crews with red and green crepe paper, there were special programs at church and school, and it was fun singing carols in the school chorus. Now if only Father could be back by Christmas, Yuki thought, everything would be almost perfect.

It was the day before Christmas and Yuki woke up feeling good. Her cot, surrounded by its monk's cloth curtain, was warm and snug, she could hear the fire crackling to life in the pot-bellied stove and the kettle on top of it was beginning to hum. Yuki

stretched and took a deep breath. Mimi's evergreens filled the
room with a good Christmas-like smell. For once she had awak-
ened before the cook pounded his spoon on the dishpan to tell
everybody in Block 7 that breakfast was ready, and she wouldn't
have to rush to the mess hall before it closed.

"You know something, Mama?" she called out over her curtain, "I have a funny feeling Papa might come back today."

Mother sounded cheerful. "I had the same feeling myself
when I woke up," she answered brightly. "Maybe it's a good
sign."

Unlike Emi's grandmother who felt good and bad signs in almost everything, Yuki's feelings rarely turned out to be much
more than wishful thinking. If she and Mother both had the
same feeling though, she reflected, maybe it *was* a good sign.
Maybe if she tried Mrs. Kurihara's system of willing things to
happen, it really might.

"Papa will come home today," she said over and over to herself. "He will. He will!"

It was like a Christmas miracle. Five minutes after they returned from breakfast, a messenger came from the Administra-
tion Office.

"Your father's back," he said as soon as Yuki opened the door.
"He's being processed and I've come to take you to the Ad
Building. Come on, let's go!"

Yuki and Ken whooped together and scrambled for their jack-
ets while Mother hurried into her coat and put on her scarf.
None of them bothered with their boots although the roads were
slushy with mud and snow. They hurried outside, gasping at the
icy wind and climbed into the truck. Ken had to sit outside in

125

back, but he didn't mind. He pulled his knit cap over his ears, shoved his hands into his pockets, and called out, "Let's go!" He would be late for work at the hospital, but he didn't care about that either.

Yuki was the first to spot Father. "Papa!" she shouted, and she ran to him, throwing herself around his neck. He was thin and he looked tired after the long trip from Montana, but he smiled happily at the sight of her.

"You're back, Papa!" Yuki shouted happily. "You're really back."

"It's been a long time," Father said as he hugged each of them. "You all look fine. Mama, you look a little thin."

"You do too, Papa San."

"And Kenichi," Father said, turning to Ken. "Have you been a good substitute for me?"

Ken grinned sheepishly. "I tried, at least for a while," he admitted, knowing that he hadn't done such a good job since coming to Topaz. "I sure am glad you're back to take over."

"And Yuki Chan," Father said, gazing fondly at her. "I believe you've grown a little."

"Half an inch up and about two inches around," Yuki informed him. "It's all the potatoes and rice and macaroni they give us in camp."

But Father didn't care if Yuki was fat or if Ken had been a poor substitute. He was back with his family after the long months of isolation in Montana, and they all knew it would be the best Christmas they'd had in many years.

That night their small barrack room was so crowded with friends and neighbors that Mother had to push back all the monk's cloth dividers so people could sit on the cots and even on the floor. All their church friends had come, and of course, Emi's grandmother. They brought cookies and candy and fruit saved from the mess hall, and Mr. Toda even produced a precious tin of coffee, telling Father that it was the first happy day he'd had since the war broke out.

Father didn't stop talking from the moment he got back. There was so much to tell about the Prisoner of War Camp where he had been interned. He told about the thirty-below Montana winter with giant icicles that ran from the roof to the ground. He told of the loneliness, even though there were thirty men in each barrack, and he told how they had kept busy with work duty and by forming all sorts of classes. He told them, too, how their mail was censored and how they could receive nothing wrapped in paper for fear that secret messages would be smuggled in.

It seemed almost like the busy happy days back in Berkeley, and Mother served tea and crackers and Spam and cheese that she had found at the canteen. She had been planning the party ever since Father's telegram arrived, and she spared nothing to make it a festive occasion.

Carolers from the church were going up and down the streets filling the night air with Christmas music, and Yuki went outside to listen to them. They sang of joy to the world and peace on earth, and at this moment Yuki felt filled with joy herself. Her own small world seemed safe and secure again, and although she knew there was no peace in the world, there seemed to be a small sliver of it in her life tonight.

She looked toward the lights of the camp hospital shining in the darkness, and thinking of Emi lying there in her cot, she hurried back inside. She found a small box and filled it with cookies

127

and fruitcake, nuts and candy, and tied a spray of evergreen on top with a red ribbon. Tomorrow she would take it to Emi, and she wasn't going to let anyone stop her from seeing her friend. In the meantime, there was still tonight to be enjoyed, and pulling up a chair, Yuki sat as close to her father as she could get.

When Yuki got to the hospital the next day, the nurse in charge was firm and unyielding.

"You may wave to your friend from the glass partition," she said crisply. "I'll see that she gets your package."

"But it's Christmas," Yuki objected. "Couldn't I go in for just a minute?"

"I'll give her your greetings," the nurse answered firmly.

Yuki knew when she was defeated. She moved to the glass partition and waved to Emi. She mouthed a big "Merry Christmas" and held up her package so Emi could see. She pointed to the nurse's back, wrinkled her nose, and said a few more things by sign language.

Emi leaned back on her pillow, giggling and signaling back. She no longer looked pale and sickly, but pink-cheeked and healthy. In fact, she scarcely looked sick at all.

"Come home soon," Yuki said, waving again, and then she left her package with the nurse and headed for home. "Merry Christmas, anyway," she called to the nurse as she left.

Yuki ran all the way back to Block 7. The north wind stung her nose and ears, but she scarcely felt it, for already she was thinking of the Christmas dinner at the mess hall. Besides that, the new red sweater that Mother had knit for her was soft and warm beneath her heavy jacket and the angora mittens from Mimi kept her fingers from getting too cold.

128

There was turkey for Christmas dinner, with as many of the trimmings as wartime rationing allowed. Ordinarily, they were each allowed thirty-nine cents a day, but Yuki knew today would be very special. The food was even served to them family style at the tables, so they needn't stand in line.

Ever since Mr. Kurihara's death, Emi's grandmother always ate with them so she now seemed part of the family. Mother had also invited Mr. Toda to have Christmas dinner with them, so with Father there and Ken eating with them for a change, it seemed almost like a holiday back home.

"I wonder what we'll be doing next Christmas?" Ken mused between mouthfuls of sweet potato.

"We'll be back home by then, I hope!" Yuki said quickly.

Ken, however, remained serious. "It all depends on the war," he answered.

It was as though he knew something that she didn't, and Yuki felt a tinge of sadness come over her happiness. She didn't ever want her family to be separated again. She wanted somehow to hold on to everybody who sat around her at the table this minute, so they would always be close and near and a part of her life. But in that circle of warmth and laughter, Ken seemed strangely silent and apart. It was almost as though he were slipping away from her already.

129

16
Another
Goodbye

$\mathcal{I}$T was in the cold bleakness of February that the army recruiters from the War Department arrived in Topaz.

"I wonder why they've come now?" Mother asked. "I thought the army wasn't accepting Nisei because of their ancestry."

"That's right, they weren't," Ken explained. "But now the Secretary of War says they want to form a special all-Nisei combat team."

"Why?" Yuki wondered. "Why can't they just join up like everybody else?"

"We'll find out if we go to the mass meeting tonight," Father said, studying the camp newspaper. "It says questions will be answered by the recruiters at Dining Hall 32."

The army recruiter who stood in front of the group was handsome in his neatly pressed uniform and his sun-bleached hair. He told them how the President felt that all loyal Americans regardless of race should be permitted to exercise their responsibilities as citizens.

131

"Why didn't he say that before we got evacuated?" a voice asked.

But the recruiter went on, explaining why the army felt a volunteer all-Nisei unit would be successful. "As a special unit they would stand out," he told them. "They wouldn't simply be additional manpower dispersed throughout the regular army, but could prove their loyalty as a special group in a very dramatic way."

Some people were nodding, but others were shaking their heads. The room was filled with the murmur of voices as people agreed or disagreed with the recruiter. Questions rained down on him from all directions.

"How do we know the Nisei unit won't simply be used as cannon fodder and sent to the most dangerous zones?" someone asked.

"Why isn't the army forming all-German and all-Italian units?" another pressed. "They're enemy countries, too."

"Why should our boys be asked to fight for a country that has put them behind barbed wire?" an elderly voice questioned. Yuki was startled to see that it was Mr. Toda who had spoken.

"I'd volunteer if I could serve like any other American," one boy said, while another favored the army plan. "It's a good way to prove our loyalty once and for all," he said. "I'll volunteer."

Yuki listened nervously as the voices grew heated with excitement. Everyone was tense and anxious, and when the meeting finally ended, everyone still seemed confused and unsure. It was difficult to know what the right decision should be. The people were filtering out of the hall, still discussing the pros and cons of the idea that had been put to them by the recruiter.

132

Mr. Toda caught up with Yuki and her parents and walked with them to the firebreak.

"Well, what do you think?" he asked Father anxiously. "What are the boys to do?"

Father was silent for a while, and then he spoke slowly. "Each man must decide for himself, Toda San," he said. "It is a difficult decision to make. But if I were young and a citizen of this country, I think I would do as my country asked. I think I would volunteer."

"Even though your country put you behind barbed wire and treated you as an enemy prisoner first?" Mr. Toda pressed.

Father nodded. "Even so," he said. "It is true this country has made a terrible mistake, interning its citizens without even a fair trial. But now it is asking for help and there isn't time to waste. Yes, I think if I had to choose, I would go, in spite of everything. I would have to make that decision."

Mr. Toda shook his head and stopped as they came to the firebreak where he would turn south and the Sakanes to the north.

"You are a good man, Sakane San," he said. "You are wise and brave and your heart holds no bitterness. Mine, alas . . . well, it is a problem that tears at the soul. I am glad it is a decision I do not have to make." He wished them a good night then, and shuffled slowly in the darkness toward his own block.

"Poor Mr. Toda," Mother said.

Mr. Toda who had always been so strong and sure of himself seemed confused and bewildered by everything that had happened since the war broke out. He was torn between two loyalties. He could no longer feel proud to be a Japanese and yet he could not become an American because a law forbade it. He was like a ship cast adrift with no ocean to sail and no safe harbor to turn to.

Yuki looked at Father now and asked her own question that had been troubling her since the meeting began.

"Papa," she said, taking his arm. "Do you want Ken to volunteer?"

Father was silent and had no ready answer as he did for Mr. Toda.

"Do you?" Yuki asked again.

"I want Ken to do whatever he feels he should do," Father said. "It's a decision he must make for himself."

Yuki turned then and looked at Mother, but she didn't have to ask what she felt. She could tell by the sad look on Mother's face that she didn't want Ken to go.

By the time they had reached their barrack, Father was talking about the coal shortage that was facing the camp, but it was really of Ken and not the coal that each of them was thinking.

Even after Yuki had crept into her small cold cot near the window, she couldn't stop thinking about the army recruiter and what he had said. She thought of what Father had said too, but she wasn't at all sure that she agreed with him. She closed her eyes tight and tried to put herself inside Ken's skin. Would she have the courage to volunteer? She curled her toes and shuddered at the thought of going to war and killing other people. Of course she couldn't do that, and she didn't want Ken to either. She wished he would hurry home so she could tell him so, but long after Yuki had gone to sleep, Ken was still out talking with his friends and thinking his own turbulent thoughts.

In the morning, Yuki saw that Ken's bed hadn't even been slept in.

"I'm afraid he and his friends have much to think about," Mother said, looking worried.

When, at last, Ken did come home, his mind was made up. "Jim and I are volunteering," he said. "We've decided it's the right thing to do. It's the only way we can prove we're as loyal as any other American."

"But what about school?" Yuki asked immediately. "I thought you were going out to college. How will you ever become a doctor?"

"College will have to wait," Ken said briefly. "There comes a time when you have to stand up and be counted for what you believe in, and I've got to go."

Ken looked anxiously at Mother and Father, not quite sure what their reaction would be, for he knew Jim's father was dead set against the whole idea. Father, however, had already put out his hand.

"I'm proud of you, Kenichi," he said firmly. "I think you and Jim made the right decision."

Mother's words were slower in coming, and Yuki was sure that deep down she didn't want Ken to go to war if he didn't have to. She looked at her hands clenched together in her lap and said quietly. "I do not like to see you go, Kenichi, but if it is your decision, I will not stop you." And then, looking up, she added, "I am proud of you too."

It all happened quickly. The army had reached inside the barbed-wire fence it had built and took Ken and Jim and hun-

135

dreds of other young men who decided to volunteer. When their papers were processed and clearances issued, the volunteers were ready to leave for basic training camp in Shelby, Mississippi.

Until almost the very last moment, Mr. Toda tried to dissuade Ken. "Do not be hasty," he cautioned over and over again. "Your very life is at stake."

But Ken had made up his mind and he would not change it.

At last, the night before Ken was to leave, Mr. Toda came with all their other friends to a farewell party for Ken. He took Ken aside and said simply, "Do you know, Kenichi, I believe you boys are doing what is right. Someday all the Nisei are going to be proud and grateful for what you are doing. You are right and I was wrong." It was a great admission for the strong-willed old man, and Ken looked pleased.

"Thanks, Mr. Toda," he said, grinning. "I'll remember what you said."

Yuki looked admiringly at her older brother. He seemed strong and brave and, somehow, suddenly grown up. The bitterness inside of him appeared to have burned away, and it was as though he had finally found himself again.

"When you do what you know is right," Father explained, "you find a dignity in yourself that makes you a happy person."

"Uh-huh," Yuki mused. "I guess Ken grew up."

There was something different about him, and although in some ways he seemed farther from her than in the days when they used to wrestle all over the floor in Berkeley, still he seemed closer to her now in an entirely different sort of way.

The boys looked sad and eager and young and brave as they climbed into the dusty buses that would take them to the railroad station in Delta. They smiled and waved to the crowd of family and friends that gathered at the gate in the afternoon sun to see them off. The Boy Scout Drum and Bugle Corps played and everyone shouted last minute words of advice.

"Take care . . . keep well . . . be careful . . . don't forget to write!"

The buses started with a roar and then went out of the gate in a cloud of dust. Yuki waved with Father's big white handkerchief until Ken's bus was just a small black spot in the road that divided the desert sand.

Already the afternoon wind was sweeping in from the desert and held the threat of a small dust storm. Yuki felt empty inside as she followed Mother and Father back toward Block 7. She wondered if she would ever see Ken again.

Mother looked sad too, and tired. But when she spoke, she said softly, "Do you know, I think there is a touch of spring in the air?"

Yuki sniffed and felt it too. Mother was right. Spring was coming and even if Ken was gone, Yuki somehow felt that everything was going to be all right, not just for Ken, but for all of them.

17
Hello, World

$\mathcal{Y}$UKI watched eagerly for further signs of spring, for the doctors had said that was when Emi might come home. Each morning as she walked to school, she looked at the willow saplings that had been planted along the main firebreaks. During the winter they had been laced with crystals of ice and children had leap-frogged over their sagging brittle branches until some had been broken into ragged stumps. Now, at last, however, there seemed to be faint stirrings of life in some of their branches, and Yuki watched anxiously for the first buds to appear.

She watched the big tree in front of the mess hall too, remembering how Mr. Kurihara had said it would die. What a mean trick of life, Yuki thought, if Mr. Kurihara was proved wrong. Then it would be the tree that would thrive green and leafy, while Mr. Kurihara lay dead in the bleak Utah desert.

Everyone else in Topaz seemed to be waiting for spring too, and an air of restlessness spread over the camp like an illness.

139

People were growing weary of being fenced inside their desert camp and the wish to be free stirred people into movement. Able-bodied men were getting permission to go out to work in the sugar beet farms of Idaho, college students were going out to schools in the East and Midwest, and families whose fathers could find work outside, were permitted to relocate outside the prohibited West Coast zone.

"Can't we leave too?" Yuki asked Father one day. "Do we have to stay here till the war ends?"

"I've given it some thought," Father assured her. "In fact, I've made some inquiries, but it's harder for me than others because I was released from Montana on parole."

Yuki wrinkled her nose. "You're not a criminal," she protested.

"No," Father said, "but still it means that wherever I go I must have a sponsor who will vouch for me."

If only they could go back to California, there would have been dozens of friends willing to sponsor Father, but the entire West Coast was still closed to all Japanese, and California did not want them back. In fact there were groups that were talking of keeping them out forever or even deporting them to Japan.

"It doesn't seem fair," Yuki said dismally. "You haven't done anything wrong."

Father nodded. "Many things in life are unfair, Yuki," he admitted, "but you must remember we're in the midst of a war and for the duration I'm an enemy alien on parole."

Yuki decided that for the time being, she would just have to stop thinking about going out, and Father continued to work in the business office with the Caucasian administrators. He was also a deacon at church, he worked on the hospital committee, and he helped their block manager iron out the problems that arose from having people living too close to one another. Father was a great peace-maker and could often smooth out difficulties between two quarreling families when no one else could. Mr. Toda sometimes said that if Father wasn't such a good business man, he would have made a wonderful minister, and Yuki thought he was right. Father was always helping other people, and he helped dozens of Issei fill out forms to get out of camp now that those with jobs or a definite place to go were permitted to leave.

"Don't you want to leave camp?" Yuki asked Mother.

"Of course I do," she answered, but she was like Father. "As long as your father can be useful and helpful in camp, I don't mind staying," she added.

Sometimes Yuki would talk to Emi's grandmother about leaving, but Mrs. Kurihara just shrugged. "Where in the world could we go?" she asked.

Emi's grandmother was going to an English class so she could learn to speak English well enough to find a job as a housekeeper if she had to. But Yuki knew her heart wasn't in it, for her dreams always revolved around her little shop in San Francisco, and that was where her spirit's longing always returned. Maybe if Mrs. Kurihara just hoped hard enough, Yuki thought, she might one day be able to buy her shop back.

One warm afternoon, when the sun was gentle and there wasn't a trace of wind, Yuki stopped by at Mrs. Kurihara's room on her way home from school. She knocked three times as she al-

141

ways did, and waited for the old woman to come to the door. She thought she heard voices and light laughter inside and almost turned to go. She didn't want to get caught up with Mrs. Kurihara's visitors and have to stay for tea with them.

When Mrs. Kurihara came to the door, she was beaming with pleasure. "Yuki Chan!" she exclaimed. "I have a surprise for you!"

And there, sitting on the army cot, surrounded by pillows and blankets, and wearing the red dress her grandmother had made was Emi, smiling and waving. "Look," she said happily. "I'm home!"

Yuki ran to Emi and gave her an enormous hug. "You're back!" she said unbelieving. "They finally let you come back!"

Emi nodded happily. "And I'm healthy now too! The doctor said I could go back to school in a few more months."

Yuki was so excited, she even forgot to sniff Mrs. Kurihara's tea to make sure it wasn't brewed from earthworms. In fact, she scarcely tasted the chocolate cream-filled cookies that Mrs. Kurihara had been saving for Emi's return. She stuffed them happily into her mouth, chewing and laughing and talking all at once.

Now that Emi was home, life seemed better. It was as though one gap in her life had been properly filled, even though there was still the one left by Ken. With Emi back, Yuki decided she could even put up with staying in camp until the end of the war, and she no longer gave much thought to leaving.

One night just after Yuki had gone to bed behind the monk's cloth hanging that separated her cot into a little corner of its own, Yuki heard a loud banging on the door. It sounded like an emergency and she held her breath as she listened to Father go to the door. A man was shouting in angry and agitated tones.

"Let's go outside and talk," Father said calmly. "My daughter has already gone to bed." And then their voices became muffled, but still, Yuki could tell the man was angry. In fact, he sounded threatening. After a while, Father came in, closing the door quietly behind him.

"What was it?" Mother whispered.

"One of the agitators," Father whispered back.

For several weeks now the entire camp had been upset by a small group of bitter, frustrated, and fanatical men who seemed to hate everybody, especially those residents who worked with the Caucasian administrative staff. They were trouble makers who roamed the camp at night, beating up the people who worked hardest as leaders of Topaz. As in any other large community, Topaz had its share of thugs.

Yuki sat up in bed, straining to listen as Mother and Father talked. Finally she got out of bed and asked, "Who was it? What did he want?"

Father brushed her questions aside. "It was nothing, Yuki," he said. "Go back to bed. Go to sleep." And after that, Mother and Father spoke in such low voices that Yuki could hear no more.

By morning the incident seemed blurred and didn't frighten her as it had at night. After all, Father had said it was nothing.

That evening, however, Mr. Toda came to visit them as he did each week. He looked worried, and for the first time since Yuki had known him, he forgot to bring her something. Tonight he seemed almost as upset as he was the night Emi's grandfather had been shot.

"There is talk that you are on the blacklist too, Mr. Sakane," he said to Father, not even bothering to lower his voice. "They say the fascist gang plans to beat you up because you work too closely with the Caucasians. They say . . ."

He was about to say more, but Father stopped him by glancing quickly at Yuki who sat on her cot trying to do her homework. It was too late, however, for she had already heard.

Mr. Toda didn't seem concerned even if Yuki had heard, for what he had to say couldn't wait. "You must take immediate steps to get out of camp," he urged Father. "What good would it do anyone if you were to be beaten up or even killed by such stupid men?"

Father looked troubled. "It is not so simple for me to leave," he said slowly. "Besides, I am doing some useful work here and I refuse to be intimidated by these gangs."

The old man shook his head and slumped down into a chair beside the stove. "What a terrible thing," he said sadly. "Fear and hatred put us into this desert camp and now we are breeding more fear and hatred among ourselves. Why must human beings be so stupid?"

Mother made some tea to ease the old man's burden and to hide her own fear. "Have some tea, Toda San," she said warmly. "Have some homemade cookies that Mrs. Jamieson sent us."

But none of them was much cheered by the tea or the cookies, for they each knew that the old man was right.

Three nights later Yuki woke up to the sound of crashing glass. Something had been flung through their window and soon a terrible smell filled the room.

Father was up in a second. "It's a stink bomb," he said, sound-

145

ing disgusted. Then he added, "Well, it's a nuisance but it didn't hurt any of us."

But Mother had finally had enough. "It's a warning, Papa San," she said. "I've made up my mind. We must leave camp. We cannot wait until something worse happens to you. We must think of ourselves now and we must think of Yuki."

Father did not argue with her. "I'll see what I can do," he said quietly.

After that everything happened so quickly that Yuki scarcely had time to think. It was arranged for Father to get special clearance to go out to Salt Lake City which was the nearest big city to Topaz. He was to report to the parole officer of the Immigration Office and Reverend Wada put him in touch with the minister of a small Japanese church there.

Father seemed excited now at the prospect of leaving. He looked at Yuki and Mother. "We won't know anyone in Salt Lake City," he said, "and I'm not sure what kind of work I can find. Are you willing to go out and try to make a go of things?"

"Sure," Yuki answered quickly, even though she was a little disappointed that they weren't going somewhere exciting like New York City. But it was hardly the time to speak of such things. "Sure, Papa," she said again.

Mother nodded too. "Of course," she said. "We'll manage. Everything will be fine as long as we're together."

It was decided that they would move to Salt Lake City as soon as they could get ready. Their life in Topaz was coming to an abrupt end and once more it was time to dismantle their room and pack their belongings.

The one thing that bothered Yuki was leaving Emi and her

grandmother behind. "Can't we take them with us?" she asked.

But even as she asked, Yuki knew it was impossible.

"We must go out first and get settled," Father explained. "Then if I can find a job and a place for them to live, we might call them out to join us."

"And Mr. Toda too," Mother added anxiously.

All of them knew how sad it was going to be for him to be left behind. He was one of the old and the young and the weak and the ill who would have to stay behind, waiting in the desert camp for the war to end.

"We'll find a way to get you out too," Yuki promised Emi. "Papa said we could call you as soon as he gets a good job."

Emi looked down at the floor, her lashes fringed with tears. "Sure. OK," she said. But her voice was so small, Yuki barely heard it.

Her grandmother was more cheerful. "We'll be all right," she said to Yuki. "Don't you worry about us. I've got all my herbs and powders and my essence of egg yolk to keep us healthy. And who knows, maybe the war will end soon and we'll all be back in California and I'll buy back my shop somehow. Then I'll invite you to the best Japanese dinner you've ever had in all your life!"

Yuki gave Mrs. Kurihara a big hug. She was full of warmth and joy and would never let the hardships of life defeat her.

Perhaps because he was older and he was all alone, Mr. Toda seemed to have run out of hope. He had no one and no home anywhere except for his cot in the Bachelors' Quarters. He seemed filled with sadness when Father told him they were leaving camp. Still he nodded and said, "It is for the best. I'm happy for you." And he asked Yuki to write to him from time to time.

147

"We'll keep in touch with you, Toda San," Mother promised. "Don't worry, we'll never forget you. Perhaps someday we can help you come out to Salt Lake City too." And she made a package of all the canned food she had on her shelf and gave it to the old man.

As soon as she knew that they were definitely going to Salt Lake City, Yuki wrote to Mimi and to Mrs. Jamieson, and the day before they were to leave an airmail package arrived for her from the Nelsons and Mrs. Jamieson.

"We want you to look very special on the day you leave for your new home," it said on the gift card. And inside the box was a beautiful pale blue dress with a matching velvet bow for her hair. It was the first new dress Yuki had had in a year. She put it on and whirled around the room. It was as though Mimi and Mrs. Jamieson were going with her to Salt Lake City, and it gave her a good warm feeling to think she had this link with her old friends in Berkeley as she left for another new home.

They all came to the gate to see them off—Mr. Toda, Emi and her grandmother, Reverend and Mrs. Wada, their church friends, Father's friends from the business office, and some of Yuki's classmates. They stood in a cluster in the hot sun, trying to look cheerful and to cover up their tears.

Yuki felt strange being the one to climb onto the bus clutching the precious pass that would let her out of the gates.

Mother bowed to everyone, Father shook hands, and Yuki hugged Emi and her grandmother and all her friends.

"Be careful . . . write . . . thank you . . . goodbye . . ."

It was like the morning they had left Berkeley, but this fare-

148

well somehow seemed sadder. Yuki blinked back her tears as she
looked out the bus window, seeing her friends blown by the
wind, holding handkerchiefs to their faces and waving . . . waving . . . waving.

"Goodbye Emi. Goodbye Mrs. Kurihara. Goodbye Mr. Toda.
Goodbye . . . goodbye."

Yuki waved and waved as the bus lurched down the dusty
road. She kept waving even when she knew her friends could no
longer see her and they became small black dots in the sand. She
watched the black barracks and the hospital and the watchtowers
grow smaller and smaller, until soon they were only a splotch in
the desert.

At last, she turned around in her seat to look ahead down the
road. Before long, trees began to appear, then green shrubs and
farmlands and lawns and flowers. And then they were in town,
driving down paved streets, going past stores and restaurants.
There were children with dogs and bicycles. There were traffic
signals and the sound of cars honking their horns.

After one long dreary year, they were back in the world again.
Yuki took a deep breath. It felt good. Her spirits began to soar,
and she looked at Mother and grinned. Maybe this wasn't Berkeley or San Francisco, but it was outside the barbed wire, and
she'd never have to live through another dust storm.

It was as though she were seeing the whole world with new
eyes. The colors seemed brighter, the air seemed fresher, the
sounds sharper. It was as though she had climbed out of a co-
coon and suddenly discovered the sun.

"Hello, world!" Yuki said brightly.

It was good to be back.